Honourable ESTATES

Honourable ESTATES

THE ENGLISH AND THEIR COUNTRY HOUSES

TIM HEALD

Illustrated by

PAUL COX

PAVILION

First published in 1992 by
PAVILION BOOKS LIMITED
196 Shaftesbury Avenue, London WC2H 8JL
Text copyright © 1992 Tim Heald
Illustrations copyright © 1992 Paul Cox

Designed by Janet James

The part lyrics from *The Stately Homes of England* by
Noel Coward are used by permission © 1938
Chappell Music Ltd, London W1Y 3FA International
Music Publications

A CIP record for this book is available from the
British Library.

ISBN 1 85145 535 3(Hb)
ISBN 1 85145 915 4 (Pb)
10 9 8 7 6 5 4 3 2 1

Printed and bound in England by Clays

CONTENTS

INTRODUCTION

Noël Coward, in his song about what are now more often called 'historic houses', wrote these words in 1938, and though they are as stylish and funny as ever they are no longer as true:

> The Stately Homes of England
> How beautiful they stand,
> To prove the upper classes
> Have still the upper hand.

In the intervening years the survival of the English 'stately home' no longer demonstrates that the upper classes have the upper hand. If anything it demonstrates precisely the opposite. There is hardly an English aristocrat still occupying his own ancestral pile who can honestly claim that his home really is his castle in the original sense that once he pulled up his drawbridge he was as safe as houses and utterly immune from trespass. Nowadays almost every one of them is permanently at home to you and me. For a modest consideration we can wander about the Duke's gardens, scrutinize his pictures and antiques, take tea in his tea-room and, if lucky, gawp at himself as well. We who live in common or garden flats can shut the door behind us and exclude the world – Dukes included – whenever we wish.

The modern stately home owner is, as he so often protests (perhaps a shade too much), no more and no less than a custodian. He keeps his great house and estate in trust for his descendants, and for the rest of us, so that we may, albeit vicariously, enjoy the beauty and the grandeur assembled by his ancestors. England's aristocrats have the use of their ancient palaces and castles, mansions and manors, but the terms have changed.

Nowadays they share.

In many cases, of course, the families have long left and their properties have become subsumed into the National Trust or English Heritage, two admirable organizations, but both of them essentially and more or less overtly in the museum business. However tastefully and carefully they present their properties there is, inevitably, a lack of soul and even an unmistakable sadness about a house in which a family has invested hundreds of years of life and history only to make way for that impersonal thing called the state. I do not mean by this that I want those huge houses to go on being occupied in the way they were at worst, with battalions of underpaid servants, poacher-catching mantraps all over the estate, and a feudal approach which lapped luxury and ground the poor at one and the same time. But I do think that if a formula can be found whereby the old family stays on and the rest of us can enjoy their treasures, then this is the best of all possible worlds.

Because of this Paul Cox and I have tried to find historic houses more or less in private hands, even though the multitude of companies and trusts that have been created to preserve that status quo sometimes means that 'private hands' is a misnomer. In one rather poignant case we did visit a National Trust property, and not every one of our houses has been in the same family for centuries. However, as a general rule we wanted to discover and describe those places where bricks and mortar and plants and flowers most obviously mingled with flesh and blood.

In our previous collaborations – a number of newspaper and magazine projects and a book called *The Character of Cricket* – we tried to be unusual without being anarchic. We have done the same here. If an anecdote, an architectural folly or even a small advertisement in a shop window, amuses or interests us we are inclined to draw it to your attention. Doubly so with a personality, particularly when, as sometimes happens in these pages, he or she seems to be part and parcel of the surroundings, chips literally off an old block. If, however, something seems boring or pretentious we are inclined to ignore it, however 'important' it may seem to the boring and pretentious. We understand that these criteria are by definition individual, eclectic and ultimately indefinable. But we are not trying to compile just another guide or encyclopaedia. If you think like us you will sympathize. If not, not.

The houses we have dealt with all intrigued us. Some came on personal recommendation; others are well known to all – though even in these instances we have tried to tease out the unexpected and the unfamiliar. They all share a strong sense of personal family involvement and commitment. In several cases this goes back several hundred years to an ancestor of the present owner and occupant who built the house in which his descendant now lives. In one, however, the owner was a first generation buyer. It seemed to us that anyone who goes out and buys a thatched castle in Devon, particularly when he is a former bank manager, deserves to be included in a book such as this. Besides, his passion for his house and for sharing it with the rest of us is as great as that of the grandest inheritor.

Like our cricket book this is full of English character. Only the English could make such a religion out of cricket, whatever the performance on the field of play; and only the English could have effected the compromises and subterfuges, undergone the trials and hardships which have kept these remarkable historic houses more or less intact and enjoyed still by their owners as well as the rest of us. Perhaps no other country in the world has heritage quite like this; but certainly no other country in the world has gone about preserving it in this way. Only the English could have turned living on a great estate into a cottage industry, transformed an Englishman's home into everyman's castle, and managed to have their hereditary cake and eat it while leaving the rest of us grateful for the crumbs.

Ironically I am writing these words in a Scottish castle which has been turned into an international writers' retreat. I am deeply grateful that such a solution should have been found for this beautiful house high on its cliff overlooking the River Esk and that it should have so benefited me and my colleagues.

Nevertheless there is something even more magical and extraordinary about the stories Paul and I have discovered in the following pages. It is the survival of an endangered species against all reasonable odds, accomplished with style, skill and great good humour. We should be proud of them.

Tim Heald
Hawthornden Castle
Lasswade, Midlothian, Scotland

HAGLEY HALL

If it wasn't for Penny,' said the 11th Viscount Cobham, sitting on the club fender in the library under a Richardson of the poet Pope, 'you wouldn't be here.' He pulled on a cheroot. 'She's a very remarkable woman.'

Lady Cobham is certainly a tremendously live wire, a Deputy Lieutenant of the County, a Board Member of the English Tourist Board, Chairman of the Heart of England Historic Houses Association, a Governor of Bromsgrove School, President of the Birmingham Festival Choral Society, a Trustee of Thomas Corbett's Charity, an Hon. Member of the Birmingham Press Club and much else besides. Most important of all, however, she is the Mistress of Hagley and the developer of Hagley Hall Entertaining, which puts on special events at home, and an infant catering company which does the same thing away. 'Hagley Hall Functions for you,' says the legend on the side of the van parked by the wandering peacock under the imposing Palladian façade which looks west to the Malvern Hills.

Although they are open to the public on sixty days of the year, 'Functions' have now become their main source of income. When they began a few years ago it was a fairly amateur enterprise with Lady Cobham doing the cooking and the household staff all mucking in. One of their first featured the butler trying to pour wine for Princess Grace of Monaco with the cork still in the bottle and another celebrity guest becoming so drunk she fell over. Today such disasters have been eliminated by smooth professionalism. The glossy brochures have a discreet Lyttelton coat of arms on the cover with two bearded mermen and a motto saying, 'Ung Dieu ung Roy'. Underneath another motto says, 'The Stately Setting for Special Occasions since 1760'. Inside it is hard sell, – well, seductive stately sell – all the way. After some lyrical elegiacs about the rolling fields and elegant landscaped park you are hit with 'only nine miles from the centre of Birmingham, minutes from junction 3 of the M5 and just 25 minutes from the National Exhibition Centre'. Then you are told that Hagley's 'eight stunning state apartments, together with three less formal ground-floor rooms, provide a unique and exclusive setting for your conference, product launch, exhibition, business or dinner entertaining'.

The range of diversions is limitless: country house sporting day, drawing-room play, murder, Naughty Tom ('The restless spirit of Thomas 2nd Lord Lyttelton'), an

evening with Noël Coward, Regency Bucks Ball, Classical Guitar Duo or Quartet. . . .
The menus range from a simple three-course meal of soup, roast and Boodle's Orange
Fool to a five-course number with game consommé and Madeira, Highland Salmon
pickled with brandy and dill, roast sirloin, Prince of Wales pudding and a croûte of
scrambled eggs with smoked oysters. If you want to stay the night there are ten bedrooms, several with the obligatory four-posters.

This is Lady Cobham's baby, and she – attractive, blonde, charming, efficient and
highly professional – is tremendously in charge. Lord Cobham is manifestly correct.
Without her Hagley Hall would be a very different place. Indeed one feels that it
might not be a Lyttelton house at all. Old people's home; health spa; multinational
Company HQ? Who knows?

'We had sixteen brand new Peugeots in yesterday,' said Lord Cobham, with an air
of patrician disbelief. 'And there was some new champagne launch the other day.' He
shifts on the fender, blows smoke and regards his wife with an affection which
suggests that he still can't quite believe his luck.

His Lordship is cast, one feels, in a more traditional mould than his switched-on
wife. A chap had been to see him earlier that morning to discuss safety regulations.
The chap had not got very far. 'I refused to see him,' he said. 'He DEMANDED to see
me. Well, one sure way of not getting to see me is demanding it.' The nosey parker
had been sent packing. 'Make no mistake,' said Lord Cobham, 'Bureaucracy will be
the death of us.' If people ask nicely and behave like gentlemen they will – I speak
from experience – be treated with courtesy and charm. Act like a bloody peasant and
you'll be treated like one. Out on your ear and damn lucky not to get a buttockful of
twelve-bore pellet. Do as you would be done by. The attitude is forthright but hard to
fault.

Like his father, a one-time Governor-General of New Zealand and a fanatical
cricketer, the present Lord Cobham is on the portly side though not as big as his
father who weighed in at eighteen stone. He too is a cricket enthusiast and a keen
Worcestershire fan. He is not, however an unequivocal supporter of Worcester's star
import, Ian Botham. 'Johnny went to Worcester for the AGM after Botham had been
hired,' said Lady Cobham, 'wearing a suit, which he hardly ever does.'

'I was going to raise it under Any Other Business,' said His Lordship. 'I wanted to
suggest that if they were going to take on players at such expense they might be
advised in future to consult the membership first. Unfortunately as I was getting up
to speak my shoulder-blade caught the light switch and I plunged the whole place
into darkness.' Covered in confusion, he remained speechless.

When he inherited in 1977 the Hall was not in a good state. 'They'd played cricket in the Long Gallery since the nineteenth century. Alfred Lyttelton got five Blues.
He was Attorney-General and centre-forward for Aston Villa and England at football

around 1905.' He played a lot of Long Gallery cricket. One generation consisted of fifteen children and a team of them did once take on the Malvern School first eleven, though they lost. Lord Cobham himself is the eldest of eight and remarks in passing that the main reason his parents had so many children was to fill the house up.

Apart from the damage caused to pictures, windows and furniture by the hard cricket ball, there were many other effects of neglect, carelessness or plain bad luck. 'A German bomb fell on the Clent Hills and dislodged the whole of one side of the house. The heating was fairly rudimentary at the best of times, and because of the bomb every flue in the house split. It was like a South American battleship.' His grandfather, a classical rather than a scientific scholar, installed lots of lightning conductors but no one told him they had to be earthed. One in particular, on the obelisk on a hilltop overlooking the Hall, proved such a magnet during electrical storms that the top section has now been completely destroyed by lightning forks. On another occasion a man who had invented a machine for making the heating work off sludge oil and diesel persuaded his father to give the invention a try. 'No wonder the old Robin Hood boilers failed.'

'Penny, bless her heart, agreed to take on a flat in the house when my father was still going. It wasn't altogether satisfactory because we didn't really have much say in how the place was run. Or not as the case may be.'

His father died in 1977. 'My mother dropped anchor for a year, which was about par for the course, and we've been here on our own since then. My father first opened the house in the Fifties. I think he thought it was money for old rope. I remember the first day the queue stretched all the way down to the Bromsgrove Road, and my mother and father had just the old-fashioned till and a Biro.'

He sees them even now in his mind's eye on their hands and knees at the end of that first day trying to add up the takings. The spectacle clearly haunts him, even though he strikes one as too phlegmatic a character to be unduly susceptible to ghosts. It was obvious to him, and perhaps even more so to Lady Cobham, that getting as many punters as possible up the drive and round the house was not necessarily the most effective way of keeping the house in the family. Four years after he succeeded his father, Hagley attracted sixty thousand people in the hundred days on which they were open. 'The wear and tear of that number of people,' he says, 'is counter-productive.' Today the house is only open for sixty days a year and the number of visitors is about half. 'Functions' have proved more profitable and less of a strain on the house.

'Hugh Hertford was tremendously helpful, I have to say,' says Lord Cobham. It is a commonplace in this curious business that competition is not cut-throat. On the contrary. The Marquess of Hertford is master of Ragley Hall and one of the older hands in the stately home business. He had begun 'functions' in 1978 and was more than happy to pass on some tips. Ragley, however, is confusingly close both geographically and phonetically to Hagley. People often end up at one when they meant to go to the other. The most famous occasion was when Hagley hosted a gathering for Jaguar Cars. Jaguar had flown in distributors and friends from all over the world, and an hour-and-a-half into dinner the Newport Pagnell police phoned to say that they'd got the Portuguese distributor of Jaguar with them. 'Where is he?' asked Lord Cobham. The answer was that he was having dinner in the cells. Apparently his hosts had given him a brand new Jag in London and once he'd hit the M1 it had acted, in Lord Cobham's words, 'like a trumpet to a warhorse, as father would say'. He had been exceeding the speed limit by 'quite a large amount'. When the wretched man finally escaped from police custody he ended in a state of total confusion at Ragley, not Hagley.

Bureaucracy is one of the banes of Lord Cobham's life and 'functioning' has, alas, raised the bureaucracy level. People came to inspect the kitchens. They found the cellars full of tin cans stocked up by his grandmother as a precaution against wartime deprivation. There were also three bottles of 1878 sherry, half a bottle of port and three made up bottles of Bronx cocktails. In the kitchen everything was lined with forbidden lead. The health inspector nearly died. They even had to get planning permission to convert the Aga to oil. It was turned down because a bureaucrat ruled the proposed tank too unsightly.

'You can have a thousand friends in and have no fire precautions, and then you sell one man a glass of beer and you have a whole ghastly bureaucracy descending upon you. You're forced into having hideous green "Exit" signs on beautiful rococo plasterwork.'

Lord Cobham was in full and entertaining flow on the subject of bureaucrats when a servant entered left with a dog. Should he take Phoebe for a walk? 'Oh yes, please, Hobbs.' 'Shall I bring her back up, My Lady?' He shall, please. These small, courteous, formal exchanges, never cease, in a world of product launches and mass catering, to take one by surprise.

Another bureaucratic insistence is regular fire practice. At one such, says Lord Cobham, 'It was deemed sensible that I should be the fire... I went about with a notice round my neck saying "fire".' He pauses, obviously relishing the recollection. 'We did have a bomb scare once,' he continues. 'I was in the park when a chap came past me at speed. In fact I have to say he was jet-propelled. All he could say was "bomb". When I got to the house I found a whole lot of wedding guests drinking champagne on the lawn and the village fête and about three thousand people on the bank. And half the Hereford and Worcester Constabulary. Everyone was out, but suddenly I realized they might have forgotten the dogs so I ran back into the house and I heard a familiar sound coming from the pantry. Went in, and there was Dyas, my

butler, opening some tins of dog food. "Come on Dyas," I said, "there's a bomb scare." And he looked at me and he said, "Yes, my Lord, but I don't believe in them.""

In 1989 they started doing catering away from home for the first time. They even offer a £10 executive breakfast and Hagley Fizz (Champagne, Cointreau and lemonade). 'Whether the venue is an office or a stately home, a cottage or a castle, Hagley Hall Outside Catering entertains your guests with style.' It began with a friend's wedding. Hot canapés and a full lunch for four hundred. Lady Cobham says that her waiters and waitresses have to be fitter than any others in the business. This is because the construction of Hagley is such that the kitchen is on a different floor from the main dining-rooms.

No historic house owner will say that he or she dislikes having the public traipsing around his home. Not for publication anyway. But Lord Cobham does have a reservation or two.

'One of the difficulties is the huge number of charities who ask us to put things on for them. We have to draw the line somewhere, so we stick to our own charities. On the whole we don't take part in functions. We have no wish to be "dinner with the duke".

'We have a suggestion box, though I hate reading nasty things about me.' Their favourite comment was: 'You will find that tea is best made with hot water.' Also: 'Your keeper has been abominably rude.'

'That was me,' says Lord Cobham, looking pleased.

Most of my talk with the Cobhams took place in the library, which is something of a hybrid. It is described in their brochure as the first room on 'what is known as the private side of the house'. Some rooms are completely private and never on public view; others, like the Long Gallery, are really only public. The library comes somewhere in between.

It is not only a sublimely elegant, yet comfortable room, it is also a proper library with three-and-a-half thousand books. These range from a first edition of Sir Thomas More's *Utopia* and first editions of Milton, Keats and Shelley to a complete Kipling, signed for his god-daughter, Meriel Lyttelton; a complete Francis Brett Young signed by him for the present Lord Cobham, who is his godson; and a complete *Wisden Cricketers' Almanack*. This last is appropriate for a family which includes no fewer than three Presidents of MCC. The books are now immaculately catalogued and rebound where necessary. When some were damaged by water they were deep-frozen and then taken to the Atomic Energy Authority at Harwell to be freeze-dried. It worked beautifully – a fine example of modern technology rescuing ancient craftsmanship.

Above the shelves there are four famous busts by Scheemakers. These were left by Alexander Pope, whose portrait hangs over the mantelpiece, to Frederick Prince of Wales. After the Prince was killed in 1752 – tragically, by a cricket ball – he left them to Lord Lyttelton, who had been his private secretary. They are of Spenser, Shakespeare, Dryden and Milton. 'Darling,' says Lord Cobham, to his wife, 'which is Shakespeare?'

A discussion ensues. It reminds Lord Cobham of an incident years ago when he was in the house on his own and his father telephoned to say that Shakespeare was being loaned to some exhibition or other and would he give it to the carrier who would be arriving shortly. A little later a man turned up with a pantechnicon. 'I grabbed the first chap with a beard and got the wrong one,' says Lord Cobham. They only found out when it arrived in London. 'Pantechnicon had to come all the way back and try again. Jolly embarrassing.'

One curiosity in the library is the small wooden carving in the middle of the fireplace. This is Dr Keate, aka 'the Baffin', headmaster of Eton in the nineteenth century, who was estimated to have flogged ten boys a day (except for Sundays) throughout his career as headmaster. His little effigy was a terrible warning to the Lyttelton young, and Lady Cobham was all for having him removed. She was overruled by the family.

Restoration has been a continuing struggle. Only one room on the ground floor was in use when they took over. Every day a piece of porcelain is being repaired, or a picture restored. The library, however, appears in pristine condition.

'God,' says Lord Cobham, removing himself at last from the fender and proposing a whirlwind tour of the house, 'going round the house with me is fun.' Indeed it is, though he is not always a hundred per cent reliable. On one famous occasion he was half-way through some hastily improvised, entirely fictitious story about the family history when he suddenly said, 'Well, at this point I think my wife had better take over.'

His Lordship's breeziness will not be found in the official guide-book. This, for instance, very properly describes the scagliola figures in the White Hall as Bacchus, Mercury, Venus and the Dancing Faun and mentions that they are copies of those in the Pitti Palace in Florence. Lord Cobham, however, explained them all, according to family tradition, in cricketing terms. Thus this one is Bosanquet bowling a googly; this a fielder in the deep dropping a catch; and, best of all, here is a toga-clad 'Plum' Warner declaring the innings closed from his bath. When Hagley was completed in 1760, the family celebrated with a three-day house-warming party in this room.

The house is mainly the creation of George, the 1st Lord Lyttelton and has been described as 'the last of the great Palladian Houses'. When Lord Cobham gave us his quick tour he, characteristically, went round in the opposite direction to his guide-book, causing a certain jovial confusion.

'They were a remarkable bunch actually,' he says, surveying a batch of family pictures with benevolent pride. They are, in fact, one of those families whose names crop up throughout our history from the time when Elizabeth I knighted Sir John in the sixteenth century. It was he who first bought the Hagley estate in 1564. 'Cricketers, statesmen, soldiers and bishops,' says the official book. (Note the fact that the cricketers are placed first.) But that bald description hardly tells the half of it. Even the National Theatre has its Lyttelton alongside its Olivier. I remember once being given an arcane account of how the Old Boy Network functioned by its eponym, a cousin of the present Viscount, ennobled as Lord Chandos and the apotheosis of Establishment Man of the old school.

If you are doing the tour according to the book and not Lord Cobham, you will proceed from White Hall to the Library to the Boudoir, the Barrel Room, the Dining Room, the Drawing Room, the Gallery and finally the Crimson Drawing room. Each according to his taste, but I particularly like the small 'boudoir' with its recent portraits, especially the present Viscount looking raffish in casually knotted scarf and his father fierce in white tie, tails and medals. The expression is, according to his son, entirely characteristic. You can see why the Gallery was so attractive to cricketers, though it must have been an incredibly awkward wicket for batting. Look out, too, for the portrait of The Misers which the second Lord Lyttelton, a founder of the Hell-fire Club, won at cards. Just as well. His own stake was the house itself.

Is it my imagination or is there just the merest whiff of the conference hotel about the rooms? The 'Exit' signs imposed by the dreaded bureaucrats obviously don't help. They are, as the Cobhams are the first to suggest, an aesthetic abomination against their rococo backgrounds. Perhaps it is just my imagination as well as the knowledge that, however wicked the 2nd Lord Lyttelton may have been, he is not being allowed to rest in peace but is even being 'persuaded to make a ghostly appearance during the hours of daylight to help promote your product or message'. Hmmm.

About Hagley's great outdoors, however, I am unequivocal. When Horace Walpole came in 1753 he wrote: 'I wore out my eyes with gazing, my feet with climbing and my tongue and vocabulary with commending.' One can see why, for the park remains unchanged and extremely beautiful. The deer are now back (Lady Cobham warned the illustrator and me to watch out for her particular favourite buck, who was inclined to butt), and there are also woodpeckers, nuthatches, warblers and badgers among the living things as well as a prince's column, a rotunda and a spectacular 'ruined castle' among the dead.

Park apart, the gardens are nothing to shout about. On the other hand there is the cricket pitch and there is the church. Happy the house with its own church and cricket pitch. The pitch was dormant on my visit though I don't feel unduly romantic

in suggesting a little flicker of a ghostly suggestion of cricketing Cobhams and Lyttel-
tons long ago.

There has been a church here for nine hundred years though this one only dates
from the thirteenth century. It is the church of the parish and the church of the family too. Lucy Lyttelton gets a fulsome rhyming tribute from her husband George, 1st
Lord Lyttelton:

> Made to engage all hearts and charm all eyes,
> Tho' Meek, Magnanimous: tho' Witty, Wise.

'The whole object,' say the Cobhams, 'is to ensure that Hagley stays as a family
house.' To which they add the rider: 'The house is part of the community. It always
has been and it's up to the family to be out and about and contributing to the
community.'

And so, in their very different ways, they are.

GOODWOOD HOUSE

G lorious Goodwood indeed! It's a glorious house and a glorious race track and even a glorious cricket ground, where they have been playing the game since at least 1727, but that September Saturday the clouds scudded low and thick over the downs and you could barely see. The illustrator and I had been bidden to the Earl of March's private box high above the winning post but it was a gumboot and galoshes day, Barbours buttoned to the neck, Herbert Johnson hats sodden and dripping. The English, as the duc de Sully said, take their pleasures sadly and on a day such as this you see what he meant – though he may not have had racing in mind.

They have been racing informally on the Sussex Downs for centuries, but in 1800 the Duke of Richmond asked the officers of the Petworth militia to hold their annual meeting there. He was their Colonel. The following year the Duke had a formal course laid out and in 1802 the first wooden stand was erected. Since then they have been improving constantly. The most recent developments are costing a cool seven million pounds.

By the time we got there the first half was complete and the Charlton Stand Phase 1 had been formally opened by Sir Ian Trethowan, Chairman of the Horserace Betting Levy Board. It's a lavishly appointed state-of-the-art grandstand, but there's no question the best thing in it is Lord March's box. Since our visit his father the Duke of Richmond and Gordon has died and the Earl himself has succeed-ed to the dukedom. 'Every so often,' he said, in a matter of fact fashion, 'the senior member of the family dies and we all move up one.' Lord Settrington becomes the Earl of March, the Earl of March becomes the Duke of Richmond and Gordon, and the Duke goes off to Chichester Cathedral. 'My father cut a hole in the woods,' said Lord March, reflectively, 'So I can see the cathedral every morning when I shave. There are six dukes buried in it.' This must concentrate his mind wonderfully before breakfast – a daily intimation of mortality.

If you are going racing at Goodwood, even on a bleak day like the one when we were there, wangle an invitation from the boss. This is the way to go to the horses. Drinks, lunch, the best view on the course, afternoon tea, frightfully good company. From the warmth and comfort of the box even the swirling grey mists looked agreeably dramatic. It was impossible to see what was going on until the very last moment, when suddenly a cavalry charge came out of the clouds and you were witnessing the climax of 'The Mail on Sunday Three Year Old Series Stakes' or 'The Skol Lager Sprint Stakes'. Was that 'Schhh You-Know-Who' (black and white (halved), check cap, light blue sleeves)? Could that be 'Chummy's Favourite' (royal blue, white cross of Lorraine)? Well who cared when there was another cucumber sandwich to hand and a nice cup of tea or something stronger if you felt so inclined. This is the life. Duke for a day.

This particular dukedom is one of the illegitimate Charles II ones. The 1st Duke, Charles Lennox, born on 29 July 1672, was the natural son of the King and Louise de Kéroualle. Louise was originally sent to England as a secret agent by Louis XIV, but obviously changed sides. Or was working as an unusually sophisticated double agent. There's the inevitable Kneller portrait of her at Goodwood and she has a distinctly double-agent look – vivid scarlet lipstick, come-hither *décolletage* and equally provocative, though rather narrowed, eyes.

The present Duke, the one who gave us lunch while still a mere Earl, is the tenth in the line. He's lived in the house since 1969. In many ways he cuts a supremely ducal figure: educated at Eton, served in the 60th Rifles, married a Colonel's daughter. In certain other respects, however, he is not what most of us expect from the higher aristocracy. He is a sufficiently serious churchman to have been a member of the General Synod for twenty years and a Church commissioner for thirteen. Even more unusually, he is a qualified chartered accountant. Charming host in the approved Eton manner, but also runs a tight ship. 'FCA, DL' are the initials after his name – 'Fellow of the Institute of Chartered Accountants, Deputy Lieutenant.' Unorthodox.

The day after the racing he took us to the cricket. This is played, as it has been since 1727, on a field a little way from the front of the house. Luckily the weather had improved. Goodwood Cricket Club were playing Broadwater. Goodwood has a membership of about twenty-five and the standard is rated 'above village'. Our host no longer played and said modestly that he had never been much good. 'I remember once getting together a team of friends and we got out three bottles of Pomerantzen which had been brought over by the Czar. It was like fire water and we gave it to our opening bowlers who bowled very fast for three overs and then collapsed.' Lord March kept wicket standing well back, but all the same one of the batsmen contrived to hit the ball straight at him, breaking his cheek-bone. He was in Chichester Hospital for nine days.

His last appearance was in period costume in 1977, when they celebrated 250 years of Goodwood cricket with an anniversary match between 'The Duke of Richmond's XII and the Gentlemen of Pepperharrowe in the dress and under the laws of 1727'. These laws, drawn up by the 2nd Duke and the 'Pepperharrowe' captain, Mr

Brodrick, are claimed at Goodwood to be the first ever, predating anything at Lord's by many years. The wickets were set a yard further apart than today's twenty-two yards – those worried about intimidatory fast bowling might be interested in reverting to the original distance – and 'shall be pitched in a fair and even place'; catching behind the wicket was allowed, whereas earlier practice was that you couldn't be given out if caught by the wicket-keeper. Rule 14 says that 'The Batt Men for every One they count are to touch the Umpire's Stick'. And so on. There were only two stumps so it was quite usual for a ball to pass between them without dislodging the bail. All bowling was under-arm, there was no LBW and the Duke's team played in white stockings, black buckled shoes, white shirts and black jockey-style caps. They usually discarded their wigs but sometimes played in waistcoats. The umpires and scorers wore long sull-skirted coats and three-cornered hats. Magnificent but hardly cricket. The present Duke kept wicket and according to tradition wore no gloves. 'I couldn't write for a week,' he says. His grandmother was a player, too. She was a member of a distinguished wandering club – 'The White Heather Ladies.'

It's all much more conventional now. The chaps were playing in white flannels. The wicket was said to be 'a bit on the slow side', because it was originally downland turf. The pavilion is thatched and the cedar nearby was planted by the 3rd Duke in the eighteenth century. The 3rd Duke was a serious political figure who among other things founded the Ordnance Survey, propounded universal suffrage 138 years before it happened, and advocated American independence. Edmund Burke told him that he and his peers were 'the great oaks that shade a country and perpetuate your benefits from generation to generation'. Horace Walpole thought him 'intrepid and tender, inflexible and humane beyond example'. The 10th Duke says he has always regarded him as 'a beacon.' His portrait, dressed all in scarlet, was painted by Sir Joshua Reynolds, who charged him thirty guineas plus another six for a miniature.

The cedar by the pavilion is one of only sixty or seventy which survive. The 3rd Duke originally planted a thousand. He and his father also went in for planting cork trees and several of these do still survive. Duke number three is the great architect of today's Goodwood. The 1st Duke bought it as a hunting lodge for a shade over £4,000 in 1697. Originally named after a Saxon owner called Goduinus, it was Godinwood at Domesday and became Goodwood in the reign of Charles II. The original house was almost completely rebuilt by the Earl of Northumberland at the beginning of the seventeenth century, so the 3rd Duke's rebuilding was a rebuilding of a rebuilding.

Although it is generally supposed that the owner, being a strong-headed figure, would have had a lot to do with the design of the house, the two professional architects were Sir William Chambers, whose most famous building is Somerset House, and James Wyatt, his successor as surveyor of the Board of Works. Wyatt came fresh from an extravagant conversion of the Oxford Street Pantheon and his work is the more distinctive. The idea – probably the Duke's – was to turn the house into a vast octagon with a three-storey pepper-pot tower at each corner. In the event only three sides were completed. The middle section has a portico with Ionic and Doric columns. The duke only wanted local materials, so it is faced in Sussex flint, largely obscured by magnolia and other climbing things.

Wyatt also designed the incredibly opulent kennels for what the Duke's sister referred to as his 'cross and pompous dogs'. Alas, the pack of hounds was wiped out by an outbreak of rabies in 1813 and the kennels is now the Club House of the Goodwood Golf Course. I'm sure it's sacrilege but I think I prefer the kennels and the stables to the main house itself – from the outside at least. They have to be the most elegant kennels and stables I have seen.

The interior is a different matter. Pride of place belongs to the ballroom, a fabulous room stuffed with Van Dykes of royal ancestors. Amazingly, it was converted into offices after the war. They put in false ceilings and laid lino on the floor. In 1970, however, it was renovated and during Goodwood race week they revived the old custom of having proper balls in it, for Lady Ellinor Gordon Lennox's twenty-first.

This tremendous party has recreated a Goodwood tradition. The present Duke moved into the house in 1968 and set about restoring the place to all its former glories. 'We knocked down thirty rooms and decorated fifty-six.' Inevitably much of the entertaining that now goes on in the house is commercial. 'I won't appear on demand,' he says, 'And I won't do it for a fee.' The family part of the house is so well separated from the public rooms that he says he can go to bed at eleven even when a dance is in full swing and not hear a thing.

The Duke organizes this entertainment business with considerable acumen and business flair. He is not just a 'great oak', he is the Chairman of the Goodwood Group of Companies, and his corporate entertainment brochure reveals that the Anglo-American Parliamentary Association have twice met there and that among the blue chip companies who have used the house are IBM, Shell, Marconi, Gulf Oil, Esso, BP, Rolls-Royce, Jaguar, Mercedes, Renault, BMW and de la Rue. In addition to all the obvious attractions you can fly your own flag, land your plane on the estate's private airstrip and drive round the estate's private motor circuit. There's even a ninety-bedroom luxury hotel converted from the old Richmond Arms.

This was originally called the Waterbeach and until 1849 there was a cockpit opposite. Nowadays guests come for golf (an eighteen-hole course) rather than cock-fighting. It's beautifully done and tremendously luxurious with sauna and solarium. But I rather hanker after the old days and was distressed to find that the old Real Tennis court has gone, though the Duke showed me a surviving wall. I suggested he rebuilt it, but he didn't seem to think it a very good idea. I wonder if the ghost of old

Mathieson still haunts the place. He was an earlier Duke's piper-valet. He would pipe round Goodwood at eight in the morning and eight in the evening every day in full Highland fig. Most of the rest of the time he spent at the Waterbeach imbibing. He used to take the Duke's sealyham, Ginger, with him and the Duke, passing by and seeing the dog on the mat outside the front door, would raise a quizzical eyebrow and say to his chauffeur, 'Well we know where to find Mathieson.'

Those charming eccentric days are history now. Sad if, like me, you're sentimental and feel that too much commercialism is a bore. But that's ridiculous. The careful development of Goodwood in its present form has ensured that the estate is still in family hands. When the 3rd Duke inherited he had only eleven hundred acres. He managed to increase that to seventeen thousand, and today astonishingly it is still twelve thousand.

Mark Girouard, the historian, comments perfectly properly at the start of one of the Goodwood guides that country house entertaining has always been a mixture of informal and formal, of private and public. 'The many organizations and individuals who enjoy its crowded schedule can feel that they are taking part in a long tradition. Country houses are meant to be full of life and people.'

Hear, hear. Up to a point. Despite the obvious claims of the 3rd Duke as the most distinguished in the line, I have a soft spot for number two. He was married in the Hague to settle a gambling debt of his frightful father's when only eighteen. He was then whisked away on the Grand Tour for three years. On returning to London he was captivated by the sight of a beautiful lady at the theatre. On making enquiries he discovered that she was not only 'the reigning toast of London' but also his wife. They were reunited and had twelve children. At Goodwood he built a stone folly called Carne's Seat, in the grounds of which his wife and daughters built a 'Shell House' lined with sea shells sent to them by naval officers serving overseas. This Duke also had a menagerie with a lion, tiger, bears, eagles and ostriches. It was he who installed hounds at Goodwood after being given the Mastership of the Charlton Hunt by his friend the Duke of Bolton.

He sounds a card, though if he were Duke today I guess the family would quickly go bankrupt. Instead Glorious Goodwood has changed spectacularly with the times and done so with exemplary taste and shrewd business sense. And who am I to question the wisdom of a man who holds not only one but four Dukedoms? Frederick Charles Gordon Lennox, Executive Chairman of the Goodwood com-panies, is Duke of Richmond, Duke of Gordon, Duke of Lennox and Duc d'Aubigny. As he says 'Once an English Duke, twice a Scottish Duke, and once a French Duke – which surely makes me the first Duke of the European Community.'

LOSELEY HOUSE

The Loseley Jersey herd of cattle was first started in 1916. It was looking spectacularly bucolic on my visit, munching its way across the field beyond the front of the house, a light tan bovid mass like a Constable painting with a sylvan background concealing the Pilgrim's Way which runs along the ridge to the north across the valley. They did look as old-fashioned as a Constable painting, but one should not be deceived. High tech has invaded the dairy.

'BA Low-Fat Set Yoghurt' is an unusual product. BA stands for Bifidus Acidophilus. According to the label 'Beneficial Bifidobacterium longum and Lactobacillus acidophilus have long been associated with good health as they survive well in the digestive tract to promote natural healthy digestion and metabolism by maintaining the proper balance of microflora.' Major More-Molyneux (you sound the final 'x', so it's More-Mollynukes) insisted I took some home. 'Make you live longer,' he said, and then qualified this extravagant claim. The slogan on the pot says, more modestly, 'Be alive with beneficial Bifidus and Acidophilus.' The major was happy to settle for that.

The health-giving properties of this lively yoghurt are remarkable, but for me the oddest aspect of the product is that it is the only yoghurt I know which advertises a historic house on the top of the pot. A black-and-white print of an imposing gabled residence bears the legend: 'Loseley House opens Wed – Sat 2 – 5pm June – Sept.' The More-Molyneux family produce some of the most famous natural dairy products in the world. They sell in Fortnums and Harrods and smart restaurants all through southern England. The day I was there a squad of Japanese experts had been in the dairy checking on the latest Loseley research. On the debit side the Major's son, Michael, Managing Director of Dairy Products, was still bemoaning the loss of thousands of pots of hazelnut yoghurt, destroyed because of an outbreak of botulism – quite unconnected – in the North West.

All this in a house where Queen Elizabeth really did sleep. Often. Indeed she was positively proprietorial when it came to Loseley, ordering the family out of the house and into the stables to accommodate her court, and insisting that the drive be covered with straw to ease the jolting of her carriage.

The family first moved into the Manor of Loseley, in its secluded valley outside

Guildford, in the reign of Henry VII. Sir William More, the second of the Loseley Mores, built the present house between 1562 and 1568. It cost £1,640.19s.7d. Most of the stone came from Waverley Abbey near Farnham, a victim of the Dissolution of the Monasteries. There are pillars of stone from quarries at Hascombe Hill and contrasting facings of Guildford 'clunch' – a soft limestone.

It's a relatively modest-looking house nowadays, though it has known grander times. At the beginning of the seventeenth century Sir George More built a north-west wing with a chapel, a riding school and a 121-foot picture gallery. It didn't last, however, and fell into such disrepair that it had to be pulled down in 1820. There is a Victorian successor, rather more modest, tucked away in the south-east towards the moat. Today that is where the junior More-Molyneux live with their four children.

The Major himself inherited in 1946 immediately after coming back from wartime service overseas. The situation could scarcely have been worse. His father had run the place with a small group of other ranks left over from the Great War. The aged butler had been his batman, there was a transport corporal who dealt with the livestock and a pioneer sergeant who looked after maintenance. This was romantic but not efficient. There was no electricity, no central heating, not even any hot water. German bombs had shattered many of the windows and the roof leaked.

Of the seventy houses on the estate most were in a similar condition. They were all either rent free or let out for 'a few bob a week'. The farm rents were £1.10.0 an acre, and of the total 1,500 acres 160 were woodland and 200 were home farm. The lawns adjoining the house were overgrown and grazed by horses of which the Major's father was inordinately fond. There was no money in the bank and death duties to be paid. It wasn't even as if the Major knew the first thing about farming. He had no experience or training at all.

However he is one of nature's triers and one of nature's optimists. He took advice from his tenant farmers, he attended night school and he became an avid disciple of George Henderson's book, *The Farming Ladder*. Henderson preached 'Work – Muck – Thought' and 'Find an opportunity in every difficulty and not a difficulty in every opportunity.' This last, in particular, was a motto for life as much as for farming, and Major More-Molyneux made the most of his difficulties, transforming them into opportunities at every turn and getting great satisfaction from what he describes as 'real work – feeding livestock, collecting the eggs, cultivations, sugar beet singling, stooking, cocking, pitching.'

But better than work was 'the arrival of the girls and their mother'. During the war he had met a girl called Donny. She called at Loseley one day, and as a result she and her sister Sue moved into a wing of the house with their mother and became an integral part of the Loseley team. Such an integral part that it was not long before Sue married the Major. She remains the chatelaine of Loseley to this day.

> Oh boy are we tanned,
> The girls wrote during those pioneer days,
>
> For we work on the land
> And we only have baths once a week.

Forty years on, Sue More-Molyneux was still going strong. It was she who took me round the gardens, now beautifully kept, after a delicious Loseley lunch of organic quiches and salads and, naturally, exotic Loseley ices. She is the sort of avid gardener who reminds me of my mother and makes me feel pathetically ignorant. As we strode down the border alongside the moat – now full of water and of fish – she exclaimed about the various flowers and plants, enthusing like mad. Sweet peas, lilies of the valley, pinks and daisies I could cope with, but my rusty 'O' Level Latin is not up to serious horticulture.

'My father-in-law had bees,' she said, 'I was terrified of them at first, but now I have them in the orchard.' We passed a finely crafted wall with the legend: 'Rudi Aedificavit. James M-M to Sue XXV 9 Oct. '73.' The translation and explanation is that Rudi, a Latvian exile, built the wall as a silver wedding present from the Major to his wife.

Just beyond the moated garden is the modern dairy where the More-Molyneux's son Michael is in charge. He was fulminating about the official decision on the hazelnut yoghurts. 'We'll send the claim to Maggie,' he said. I wasn't sure whether or not he was joking. In 1987 Booker plc took a majority share in the Dairy Products part of Loseley, something I hadn't really taken in until I was asked to that year's Booker Literary Prize dinner by my friend and former tutor Professor Richard Cobb and found that the exotic puds at the banquet were all laid on by Loseley. 'Production remains on the estate and is run by the family,' says the Major. So let there be no mistake.

The Major's father began selling milk and butter in 1923, but although this produced a perfectly satisfactory return it wasn't until 1967 that the real Loseley revolution took place. This coincided with the arrival of a new farm secretary/book-keeper and receptionist called Daphne Holloway. She was concerned about the waste of skim milk in the dairy process and asked if she could have a go at making cottage cheese. Loseley was already supplying organically grown vegetables to Cranks, the health food people, one of whose food shops and restaurants is, fortuitously, in Guildford, just over three miles away. Cranks liked the cottage cheese and asked for more. A little later they had a problem with their regular yoghurt maker and asked Loseley to help. They liked the yoghurt too. Then Sue More-Molyneux thought it would be fun to try ice cream, so they bought a machine and started making that also.

The rest, of course, is history. The range of products is now enormous: Greek style yoghurts and Lebnie; live yoghurts with raspberry, blackcurrant, apricot, strawberry and the troublesome hazelnuts; Jersey cream, soured, whipping, single, double and revolutionary 'extra thick single' for contemporary living (the 'spoonability' of a whipped double cream but only the calories of a single); ice cream with acacia honey and stem ginger and Brazilian rum and Grand Marnier bombes and Apricot and Amaretto bombes and chocolate Mint Royal bombes and, best of all, a Mississippi Mud Pie with chocolate fudge and hazelnuts, chocolate nut fudge sauce, rich dark chocolate, coffee and old-fashioned vanilla ice cream . . . Daphne Holloway, incidentally, retired in 1989, but was made Life President of the company as a tribute to her endeavours over the years.

There's a lot of food at Loseley and after we had seen the garden Sue More-Molyneux drove me down to see more of it on the hoof. There are twenty-eight different breeds of sheep, thirty different sorts of poultry and ten different kinds of pig. Tamworths, Blue Cochins, Greyfaced Dartmoors. There is even a pedigree miniature Vietnamese potbelly boar. 'Hello woollies!' said Mrs More-Molyneux, addressing a flock of allsort sheep, who looked pleased to see her. She lowered her voice. 'I'm afraid we lost the toucan. It had a heart attack in a thunderstorm.'

Back at the house I was shown round by Mrs Quarmby, one of the regular Loseley guides. I was preceded by the group of French students who had been referred to with some apprehension during lunch. ('I thought we said we wouldn't have any more?') About ten thousand visitors look round the house every year, and slightly more go round the farm. Adults, mainly, do the house while the farm is more popular with children. Perhaps the French students would have been better off with the animals.

Me too, if the truth be told. It's not that there's anything wrong with the house but it did seem a little dark and Grinling Gibbons (he did actually do the carving on the minstrels' gallery in the Great Hall). Too much brown for a hazy hot English summer's day. The hall panelling is chocolate too. It came from Henry VIII's Nonsuch Palace when it was demolished. Nonsuch was built for one of his wives, Katherine Parr, and her initials are carved into one of the panels. So are her husband's, together with his personal portcullis.

Pride of place inside the house goes to a South German Wrangelschrank. It must be rather special because my guide said, in hushed tones, 'Getty tried to get the Wrangelschrank.' If Getty tried to get it, it must be good. Even more to the point, Getty failed. Not something to which he was accustomed. The Wrangelschrank is a sixteenth-century South German cabinet of pine inlaid with pear, rose, beech, sycamore, Hungarian ash and what the Major a touch evasively refers to as 'other woods'. Carved into the exterior is a lost city, its ruins encrusted with rampant ivies and clinging vines. It's wonderful – if you like that sort of thing.

More interesting, to my mind, is the staircase. This is hung with religious pictures culminating in 'The Living Christ, an inspired mystical picture by the Jewish artist, Berthe Hess; St Francis; St Bernadette's vision of the Virgin Mary at Lourdes; Dorothy Kerin raised from the dead in 1912, and Sue Coles, instantly healed of cancer in the 1970's.' And finally a chapel.

Hereby, clearly, hangs a tale. Over a scrumptious tea on the lawn outside the restored seventeenth-century tithe barn I got an inkling of it. The major is, well, diffident is not the word, but he doesn't want to force his views and he wasn't going to talk about God unless I was interested.

I said I was.

And here, I confess, I find myself subject to the Major's own reservations. He says that when you get to the subject of religion and say 'I'll give you more if you like', you immediately lose two-thirds of your audience. So perhaps I won't go on too long. Suffice it to say that there is at Loseley a 'Christian Cancer Help Centre'. They, a group which includes a doctor, two clergy, a nun, housewives, organic gardeners, an artist, a dietician and a blind physiotherapist, meet on alternate Tuesdays. Eight or so cancer patients turn up. There is prayer and ice cream. 'Love flows in and fear goes out,' he says.

And there, perhaps, we should leave it. It's perfectly plain that Major More-Molyneux is a religious man, and it seems to me that it's a religion that informs most, if not all, of what he does, but in saying even that there is a hideous danger of making him seem pious, proselytizing or prim. He is none of these, but the staircase seems to be the clue to the essence of his enterprise. Remember too that the stone from which his house was originally built was used in the construction of a Cistercian abbey 850 years ago. As he himself says, 'Something of the peace of those Cistercian monks remains in the mellow walls.'

Over the inner door of the entrance hall there is an inscription: 'Invidiae claudor, pateo sed semper amico.' His own translation is: 'I am shut to envy, but always open to a friend.'

It's an entirely appropriate legend for the front door of Loseley.

STANSTED PARK

E ntering the library at Stansted Park, the Earl of Bessborough's Sussex seat, I immediately experienced the curious sensation of having walked into the pages of a P. G. Wodehouse novel. There had already been a rather dizzy blonde walking though the hall who turned out to be the daughter of the American ambassador, just the sort of girl to excite a man like Wooster were she not married to the cove in the yellow cardigan who worked for a merchant bank and was standing looking out at the cricket ground. And there, slumped in an armchair reading a newspaper, was my old friend and former colleague Kenneth Rose.

Kenneth Rose is the respected biographer of Curzon and George VI as well as the inventor of the *Sunday Telegraph's* Albany column. Reading his weekly words one forms an impression, accurate in my view, of a man who does not go to the office (especially now that it is in Dockland) but spends his daily lunches (or, in Albany argot, luncheons) in St James's clubs, his dinners at high table in the smarter Oxford and Cambridge colleges, and his week-ends in large, grand country houses.

I should not therefore have been in the least surprised to find him in one of the Earl of Bessborough's comfortable armchairs that Sunday morning. Yet I did feel uneasily that I had stepped through the looking-glass into a world of Wodehouse.

Of Lord Bessborough, my host, there was at first no sign, but presently he shuffled in, beaming like a latter-day Lord Emsworth, to suggest that I poured myself a

drink. This is a characteristic hazard of country house entertaining, the first fence in an etiquette steeplechase. I opted for a dryish sherry and managed neither to spill it nor to knock over any of the close-packed glasses in the drinks cabinet. Lord Bessborough, the 10th Earl, stirred himself an exceedingly dry martini, thus managing to imply just the mildest *faux pas* on my part, rather as if I had picked up the wrong fork at lunch(eon). Presently, the illustrator, who had been staying with his in-laws at – of all places – Emsworth, entered through the French windows clutching his sketching pad and looking like a boyish Psmith. This was getting ridiculous.

Not so ridiculous as all that. There *is* a connection between Stansted Park and the immortal Plum. What is more, Lord Bessborough has a pamphlet to prove it. The pamphlet is really designed to entice you to become a 'Friend of Stansted Park.' For ten pounds a year you can help 'The Stansted Park Foundation' (est. 1983) to 'preserve the House and Park for the educational and recreational purposes of the public.' One can't, in a materialist age, avoid an unworthy suspicion that the most important aim of the Stansted Park Foundation is actually to enable Lord Bessborough, his heirs and assigns, to continue to live in these agreeable surroundings for ever and a day. But that's as maybe. As a 'Friend' you and a guest get in free every day during the season whenever you want; you can attend the monthly 'Connoisseur's Days' when you can get to the parts of the house other people cannot reach – like the library in which we were enjoying our Sunday morning drinks; you have the right to purchase Lord Bessborough's own book *Enchanted Forest – the Story of Stansted in Sussex* at a discount of £3 *and* the author 'will inscribe copies specially for Friends'; you will be notified about special events at Stansted; and you will be able to hire the restaurant at a reduced rate.

Good value for your ten pounds, but what has this to do with P. G. Wodehouse? The answer is that next to the various enticements offered in *Be a Friend of Stansted Park* there is a panel headed 'Stansted Park and P. G. Wodehouse'. This leans heavily on a book by a Colonel Norman Murphy entitled *In Search of Blandings*. The Colonel had taken seven years of his life to 'prove' such things as that the original Wodehouse's Lord Uffenham was Anthony Lejeune's uncle. One of the things he 'proves' is that Wodehouse used real-life Stansted Park as a model for such fictitious historic houses as 'Stansted House' and 'Belpher Castle', but not Blandings itself. 'Belpher Castle is Stansted Park,' writes Colonel Murphy with military certainty. I remember his book well because I had to review it for the *Daily Telegraph* and said, more or less, that recondite and diligent though it was, in my opinion the Colonel had spent seven years of his life wasting it. But there you are. What is incontrovertible is that Wodehouse bought a house called Threepwood in Emsworth in 1910.

'Another curious fact,' says Lord Bessborough, is that when he was the first British Vice-President of the European Parliament, and was responsible for earthquake relief in north-east Italy during the 1970s, the local authorities honoured him by recreating the Dukedom of Friuli for him. Those familiar with the Master's work will join Lord Bessborough in wondering if he was clairvoyant.

Not that anyone should be fooled into thinking that Frederick, Lord Bessborough is no more than a genial old buffer who has stepped unchanged straight from the pages of English farce. Certainly he is aristocratic, certainly he is the wrong side of seventy (born in 1913), and certainly he seems to cultivate a certain gentle eccentricity – I was most taken with the outsize walking stick he affected when we toured the policies that afternoon.

But Lord Bessborough is a man of parts and that still rare specimen, a man who can cope with the two cultures, having been, for instance, Minister of State at the Ministry of Technology and the author of a play, *The Four Men*, specially commissioned for the Festival of Britain. He has twice led missions to the People's Republic of China, was instrumental in setting up the first direct television link between London and Moscow, and is President of the Men of the Trees. Like many of the best aristocrats, he is splendidly unpredictable and resistant to typecasting.

Apart from being the Earl of Bessborough he is also Viscount Duncannon and Baron Ponsonby. These titles derive from the early to mid eighteenth century. The family link with Stansted, however, is comparatively recent. The ancestral home proper was Bessborough, near Waterford in Ireland. It burned down in the Troubles, but the family picture collection was rescued. The 9th Earl and his wife wanted somewhere safe to hang the pictures and drew up a long short list of suitable houses all round England. By 1923 they were down to the final sixty suitable properties and the ten-year-old Frederick was given a copy of the latest *Country Life*. In the pages at the beginning 'I saw a beautiful photograph of Stansted from the avenue and told my parents that was my choice and they agreed.' The statement is breathtaking in its simplicity but it has the ring of truth.

I was at Stansted on a Sunday because Sunday is when Stansted play cricket. Stately cricket tends to be a sub-text in this book and it is very much a sub-text in the lives of both Stansted and the Earls of Bessborough. The 6th Earl and his younger brother Spencer were founder members of the greatest of all wandering cricket clubs, I Zingari, and a famous portrait of them hangs in the Long Room at Lord's. The present Lord Bessborough was able to produce a marvellous picture of the 6th Earl umpiring at Harrow in a black coat and top hat. He never married and was a sort of perpetual schoolboy, continuing to hang around Harrow throughout adult life. His brother Spencer later became Sir Spencer Cecil Brabazon Ponsonby-Fane. Names, commented the cricket buff Benny Green, in one assessment, 'accrued to him like barnacles to the hulk of a privateer.' He was for thirty-seven years treasurer of MCC, and in 1914, shortly before his death, he was the club's oldest living member.

The present Lord Bessborough – not, on his own admission, much of a cricketer, though he liked to come in very late and biff a couple of sixes or so – showed me Sir Spencer's recommended LBW law with much enthusiasm. Quite right too. It was far too radical for 1885, when he proposed it, and would be thought far too radical today, when part of the science of batsmanship is the skilful use of different sorts of protective clothing instead of the bat. 'The striker,' proposed Ponsonby-Fane, 'shall defend his wicket with his bat only, not his person. If he shall wilfully defend his wicket with his leg or person he shall be out Leg Before Wicket.' Lord Bessborough and I agreed that this eminently sensible and practical idea should be reproposed forthwith. As we are both members of MCC we should do it ourselves, but I suspect we shall need signatures and meet tiresome 'expert' opposition.

Stansted Park Cricket Club play on the lawn outside the front of the house. At the end of a hot, arid summer it was looking like a Kipling *maidan* in Bangalore or Hyderabad, fit only for a Maltese Cat. However, a Hayling Island XI had arrived and a full afternoon's cricket was confidently expected.

They have been playing cricket here since 1741. Captain James, the Earl's agent, sent me two extracts from letters from the Duke of Richmond to the Duke of Newcastle dated 1741. On 14 June he wrote:

'Sergison was expected last night at Westdean and 'tis believed he will go to a Great Crickett Match in Stansted Parke tomorrow between Slyndon and Portsmouth. If he does I'll face him there with fifty staunch freeholders all engaged to us.'

Sergison, who was MP for Lewes from 1747 to 1766, was standing for election in Sussex against the candidate of the two Dukes. The Dukes had put up their own candidate and were none too pleased at the idea of Sergison opposing him.

Two days later the Duke of Richmond wrote again to the Duke of Newcastle, 'Sergison,' he reported, 'was at the Crickett Match attended by Lisbon Peckham, old Eastgate the hatter, Ludgater and two or three more of the Chicester Torys. He did not venture to aske a vote, nor could he have gott one I do really believe. Tanky was there ready to puff his cheeks at him, butt he never appear's before us, butt quietly stole away, as soon as we came. All our friends seem'd mighty hearty and were in great spirits especially as Slyndon beat Portsmouth, and had nine men to go in.'

Neither Slyndon nor Portsmouth appear on the modern Stansted fixture list, which ranges from local towns and villages such as Midhurst and Selsey to such typically but esoterically named sides as the Zombies, Extroverts, Rioteers, Iconoclasts and Gilbertians. Lord Bessborough is, naturally, President of the club, and presides over a powerful squad of Vice Presidents including Baroness Airey of Abingdon, Lady Ilife and the Count Lanza, who is Lord Bessborough's nephew. Perhaps he is a rock star. From time to time the ground is also host to special matches – a game in aid of Chichester Theatre perhaps, or the gala game played to celebrate the eightieth birthday of Lord Home of the Hirsel. But Lord Bessborough concedes that his interest in the game is not as keen as it once was. What he likes to do of a summer evening is to equip himself with a powerful Scotch and go outside to watch the final overs in the hope of catching a dramatic finish. 'I can,' he says, 'just, with my binoculars, see the score from the terrace.'

Stansted is unusual in having a cricket ground, particularly one which is only separated from the front door by a swathe of gravel drive, but it is even odder in boasting a theatre. The night before my visit there had been sixty or so guests for a Chekhov production mounted largely thanks to the energy of staff from Bedales School close by. The original theatre was built by Lord Bessborough's father an inadvertently burned down after a Home Guard exercise during the war.

The family's theatrical associations began, like the cricket, with the Victorian 6th Earl, and indeed cricket and theatre are inextricably muddled. The 6th Earl not only helped start I Zingari, he also gave birth to 'The Old Stagers' in 1842. This was an amateur theatrical company which put on plays during the Canterbury cricket week, at which IZ regularly performed. When the present Earl's father built his theatre in 1927, the idea was to follow the Canterbury precedent: cricket by day, acting by night.

Lord Bessborough himself was an avid thespian and he positively sparkled when we arrived in the theatre and started looking at the history of the Stansted Players between 1927 and 1938. 'I was Oberon in the *Dream*,' he says, pointing to the inaugural production in 1927. The young Viscount Duncannon (his title in those days) was a star. He played Romeo. He played Hamlet. He played Little Billee in *Trilby* and Lorenzo in *The Merchant of Venice*. In 1929 the Players staged *Henry IV Part 1*. This was a Ponsonby family triumph. The drama critic of the *Morning Post* wrote that Shakespeare himself 'would have approved the youth and mettle of the chief protagonists, Viscount Duncannon as Prince Hall [sic] and his cousin, Mr Arthur Ponsonby, as Hotspur, both of them just sixteen – the same age, it may be remembered, as that of the future Henry V when he returned from suppressing Welsh rebellion.' Every schoolboy in 1929 naturally knew that Henry V was sixteen when he put down the Welsh. The man from the *Post* went on to say: 'The fact that Lord Bessborough himself played Henry IV with quiet dignity, lent a further personal touch to this remarkable performance.' The companies were amateurs augmented by outside professionals. Dulcie Grey accepted Michael Denison's marriage proposal while playing in *The School for Scandal* at Stansted.

The Stansted Players were not revived after the Home Guard fire, but the theatre was rebuilt and the family theatrical tradition was perpetuated when Lord Bessborough turned up at Sir Laurence Olivier's dressing-room at the Century Theatre in New York, when he was playing in Anouilh's *Becket*. That was in 1960. Lord

Bessborough went off for a prolonged dinner at Olivier's apartment, and after a night poring over the plans of the proposed Chichester Festival Theatre, Olivier had virtually agreed to become its first Artistic Director. Thirty years later Lord Bessborough was still the Chairman of the Chichester Festival Theatre.

It was only because of a family tragedy that Frederick, the 10th Earl, succeeded to the title. The beech avenue which runs two miles from the house to the outskirts of Rowlands Castle is the longest in England. In 1926, two years after the family moved to Stansted, Frederick's elder brother, Desmond, fell from his horse while riding there and was killed. A plaque in the chapel records this melancholy event and also the death of another brother George, who was killed on military manoeuvres in 1951, aged only twenty.

The chapel is a mixture of Tudor red brick and nineteenth-century neo-Gothick, a small but elegant building away from the house by the walled vegetable gardens. It has an odd history and one famous association.

In 1804 Stansted was sold to an Old Etonian barrister called Lewis Way for £173,000. Way had been left £300,000 by John Way, no relation, because he, John, had no confidence in his true heir, Thomas Way. When John invited Thomas to dinner and had trouble opening the port, Thomas came to his aid by fishing a corkscrew out of his pocket. Far from being grateful, old John decided that any man who walked around with a corkscrew in his pocket was a bad lot and not fit for his fortune. Later he noticed the name Lewis Way outside the door of Chambers in the Temple, walked in and offered Lewis his fortune. He had never seen him before in his life. John and Lewis were both committed Christians and it was agreed that the new heir would devote his fortune to setting up some sort of religious institution. After more than six years' thought Lewis decided that his life's work was to be the conversion of the Jews to Christianity and their return to Palestine. He accordingly founded a Hebrew College at Stansted, but this failed when sixteen young Jews staying in the house heard the false rumour that Way was bankrupt and absconded with the family silver. Macaulay celebrated the incident in verse:

> Each says the proverb to his taste. 'Tis true
> Marsh loves a controversy, Coates a play,
> Bennet a felon, Lewis Way a Jew,
> The Jew, the silver spoons of Lewis Way.

Way's next scheme was to persuade Tsar Alexander I of Russia to campaign for getting the Jews back to Palestine. He travelled to Russia and met Alexander, who was sufficiently sympathetic to allow him to plead the cause at the Congress of Aix-la-Chapelle in 1818. Despite an audience which included Castlereagh, Wellington, Metternich and Nesselrode, nothing much came of this and Way returned to Stansted

disillusioned but just in time for the consecration of a much enlarged and redecorated Tudor chapel.

That's the oddity. The celebrity is Keats, the poet who was staying nearby at Bedhampton while working on 'The Eve of St Agnes' and 'The Eve of St Mark'. Reading about the impending consecration in the local paper, Keats and his friend Brown decided to attend. 'Tomorrow,' wrote Brown, 'we shall go to Stansted [sic] to see Mr Way's Chapel consecrated by the two Bigwigs of Gloucester and St David's.'

In a letter to George and Georgiana Keats, the poet said, 'The consecration was not amusing. There were numbers of carriages – and his house [Way's] crammed with clergy. They sanctified the chapel, and it being a wet day, consecrated the burial-ground through the vestry window. I begin to hate parsons; they did not make me love them that day, when I saw them in their proper colours. A parson is a Lamb in a drawing-room, and a Lion in a Vestry.' However he may have disliked the occasion it seems certain that Keats drew extensively on the experience and the building itself when he returned to writing his two poems. Anyone sufficiently interested should study the text and visit the building, then, as they say in academic circles, 'compare and contrast'.

We toured the house and grounds, discursively and slowly that afternoon, a stately progress peppered with 'Good Afternoon, My Lords' courteously acknowledged with a wave of the walking stick, a brief reminiscence, an occasional autograph. We watched cricket for a while and saw the batsmen struggle. We sucked teeth over the devastation of the arboretum and park in the great storm. We were grateful that they hadn't replanted too much because the young trees wouldn't have weathered the summer drought. We gossiped about everything from the 'Drunken Duchesses with their flat bottoms', in which Lord Bessborough sailed to Canada when his father was Governor-General, to the time when Lord Hailsham and he entertained the first woman astronaut to go into space. She was Russian and rather pretty. He told me about how he used to play mah-jong here with the Princess Royal and how he had to be strangled once in a play called *The Cat and the Cherub*. And then it was time for afternoon tea in the library under the splendid John Piper of Chichester Cathedral which some people join 'The Friends' specially to see – the painting not being on show to the general public. And after tea Kenneth Rose and the young Americans set off back to London and somehow tea merged into drinks. There had been a terrible fire at another great Sussex House, Uppark, and a desolate member of the owners' family had called for consolation. It reminded Lord Bessborough that Stansted too had been almost destroyed in a great fire in 1900. It lasted from eight one night to six the next morning. The Grinling Gibbons carvings went up in smoke, and so did the Italian frescoes and the portraits of Queen Elizabeth and Queen Mary in the room in which they both once slept. The house was rebuilt by Arthur Conran Blomfield Jnr in 1902, with the same proportions but a different appearance. To judge from the photographs, Blomfield's house is an improvement on its predecessor.

A great debate was raging about what to do with the burned-out shell of Uppark. We debated this. To restore? To rebuild? To demolish? To abandon? You could make a case for all these. And then we shuffled on to the terrace with our drinks and Lord Bessborough fished out his binoculars and we peered towards the front lawn where, as the shadows lengthened, the run makers flickered to and fro just as they have been doing since that summer day in 1741 when poor Sergison was frightened by the Duke of Richmond and his eighteenth-century bully boys.

And finally, shortly before stumps, I too, like Sergison, quietly stole away.

BEAULIEU

For once in his own bailiwick Lord Montagu was not the centre of attraction. As my train pulled into Brockenhurst from Waterloo it was his son, the Hon. Ralph Douglas-Scott-Montagu, who was clutching a sheet of paper and looking mildly apprehensive as he chatted to a series of British Rail bureaucrats. Lord Montagu himself was on the outskirts of the throng, snapping photographs. Anyone who didn't know him might even have been guilty of the ultimate heresy and mistaken him for a member of the general public.

The Hon. Ralph was naming a buffet car. Some seven years earlier he had written to BR suggesting that they revert to their old tradition of calling their trains after the great and the good or the old and the bold. Now, with their customary alacrity, BR had agreed to name one of their new Wessex Electric Fleet 'Beaulieu' and, very properly, they had asked the younger Montagu to perform the ceremony. British Rail were out in force, and there was a man from the *New Milton Advertiser* to record the occasion. Other members of the family present included Ralph's mother Belinda, Lady Montagu and his grandmother, the indefatigible 94-year-old Mrs Edward Pleydell-Bouverie who, in an amused stage whisper, expressed some misgivings about the new-fangled rolling stock which she found less comfortable and convenient than the old. Entering and alighting are apparently not easy for the aged.

Like practically everyone else in the world I have always associated Beaulieu and Lord Montagu with the motor car. Had not the present Lord Montagu's father introduced King Edward VII to the joys of motoring? Was not the National Motor Museum built on Lord Montagu's estate? And was not Lord Montagu its onelie begetter? Yes to all three – and yet there are railways in the family tree as well. When the Hon. Ralph delivered his formal speech he revealed that his grandfather had qualified as an engine driver in 1888. He did so under the commoner-sobriquet, 'Mr Douglas', engine driving not being a pursuit generally favoured by the nobility.

One sensed a certain filial pleasure in Lord Montagu's son being able to demonstrate that the family's devotion to steam preceded its love affair with the internal combustion engine. The Hon. Ralph was not exactly cocking a snook at his famous motoring father, but he was demonstrating, in the nicest possible way, that like father, not necessarily like son.

I have a particular interest in Beaulieu because in 1966 I helped Lord Montagu with a book called *The Gilt and the Gingerbread*. The title is a quote from Noël Coward's 'Stately Homes of England' and was suggested by my mother. The subtitle, though starker, is more explicit: 'How to live in a stately home and make money.' I was working on the Atticus column at the *Sunday Times* in those days and Lord Montagu's preferred choice for hired help was my boss Hunter Davies. Hunter was too grand even then – his novel had been filmed, he'd been commissioned to write a book about the Beatles – but with characteristic magnanimity he suggested me. The book was so successful that I was able to buy my first new car with it – a scarlet Mini, Reg PGH 726E. If it's still alive it really ought to have a little niche in the Motor Museum.

By that time Beaulieu was already a success, though not on the scale it is now. Lord Montagu had opened the house for the first time in 1952 shortly after succeeding to the estate at the age of twenty-five. Opening was by no means a foregone conclusion, although it was obvious that something had to be done as the house was far too expensive to be maintained from the estate income. A few years earlier Montagu had been in such despair that he had offered the house to the Bishop of Winchester as a home for retired clergy, provided he could keep on a flat in the building for himself. Odd to think that he might have spent his life as a sort of sitting tenant surrounded by minor canons instead of becoming arguably the most successful impresario in the business.

By the time he succeeded, however, he was feeling more brave and resolute. Other historic house owners – notably Lord Bath at Longleat and the Duke of Bedford at Woburn – had shown that with a bit of flair and business acumen you could make a go of opening to the public. Besides, there was a tradition at Beaulieu where, in 1951, no less than forty thousand people had paid a shilling a head to see round the Abbey ruins. Before the war they had even sold souvenirs – model monks hand made by a friend of Lord Montagu's father's secretary.

However, as he is the first to admit, rivals like Bath and Bedford had one insuperable advantage. They each owned a palatial house stuffed with artistic treasures. Attracting the punters to houses like that was simplicity itself. Unlike them, Montagu has always conceded, 'It was not enough to put up a notice in the village saying that anyone who wanted to could come and look round Palace House and its garden for a shilling. Frankly, it was not and is not that sort of house.'

The Motor Museum was what made the difference. Like most brilliant ideas it seems in retrospect to be so obvious as to be inevitable. No one had tried to establish one since Edmund Dangerfield at the Crystal Palace in 1912. His collection was dispersed during the First World War. For Montagu it was not just a commercial stroke of genius, it was also a worthy memorial to his father, one of the great pioneers of

British motoring. He was the first Englishman to race a British car on the Continent; he introduced the Prince of Wales to the Daimler in 1899; he was responsible for the 1903 Motor Car Bill which made number plates compulsory and raised the speed limit from 12 to 20mph. This last was a satisfactory revenge on the Basingstoke magistrates who, a year earlier, had found him guilty of going faster than 12mph and had fined him £5 'to mark the seriousness of this breach of the law.'

This summons was one of the original exhibits in the first museum which was located in the front hall of the house itself. The cornerstone was Montagu's father's 1903 De Dion Bouton, which had been used by the estate electrician for a number of years and was very much the worse for wear until Montagu himself personally stripped it down and painted it bright green. In addition he persuaded various car makers to lend him early models, so that by Sunday 6 April 1952 he had an 1899 Daimler, a Beeston Forecar, Quad and tricycle all dating from 1896, a 1901 Sunbeam Mabley designed to be driven from the rear seat, a 1905 Vauxhall, a 1906 Lagonda personally loaned by David Brown, and an 1899 Benz and an 1896 Léon Bollée loaned by two local well-wishers.

It all sounds wonderfully English, amateurish and old-fashioned, though one should not be altogether deceived. As befits someone who not only worked in PR (he was a director of Voice and Vision, a subsidiary of Colman, Prentice and Varley) but was also once on the *Daily Express*, Lord Montagu has a flair for publicity. He was always ready with an apt quote, such as: 'I would rather keep my home and surrender my privacy, than have things the other way round.' He was good at photo opportunities such as the one of him on hands and knees with a scrubbing brush – 'It's enough to bring a Peer to his knees' (*Sunday Pictorial*) and 'Seine Lordschaft schrubbt die Boden'. They had seven thousand visitors that first Easter and they have never, I think it's fair to say, looked back.

By the mid 1960s, when I first met him, Lord Montagu was a celebrity, if not an institution. He was, I suppose, best known for the Motoring Museum, but it's strange how public perceptions have changed over the last quarter of a century. If you were playing word association games then and now the first thing you'd say in response to the word 'Montagu' would probably be 'old car'; but in those days you'd be almost as likely to say 'Jazz festival'. Nowadays few even of the middle-aged would think of Jazz apropos of Montagu. You'd be much more likely to say 'Heritage'. In those days, of course, he was barely forty and widely regarded as a bit of a swinger. Now he is in his mid sixties and has acquired gravitas.

The Beaulieu Jazz Festivals ran from 1956 to 1961 and they were famous in their day. The first was a very modest affair organized in conjunction with the Yellow Dog Jazz Club in Southampton. The star turn was the Avon City Jazz Band from Bristol. After that, however, it growed like Topsy until by year five they were predicting an

attendance of at least ten thousand. The twenty-one bands engaged included Acker Bilk, Johnny Dankworth, Tubby Hayes, Nat Gonella, Ronnie Scott, Humphrey Lyttelton and the Americans Memphis Slim and Little Brother Montgomery.

The 1960 jazz festival became known as the Battle of Beaulieu. Too few police, too much beer – 330 gallons of draught and 24,000 bottles at the Montagu Arms alone – and a serious feud between the followers of 'Modern' and 'Traditional' jazz ended in complete chaos. 'Pandemonio di 8,000 Giovanni,' thundered the Italian press, while in the *New Statesman* John Freeman waxed hugely indignant about the inadequate lavatories. A year later the festival, augmented by Chris Barber, Kenny Ball, Mick Mulligan with George Melly and Anita O'Day, fresh from her success at the Newport Jazz Festival, went off without a hitch. Acker Bilk was considered too provocative to be on the bill. Outside the grounds, however, there was even worse 'pandemonio' than the year before. At the end of the festival Lord Montagu called all the bands on stage for a final version of the 'Saints'. It was a Last Post. 'I would like to have gone on, year after year, but the hoodlums defeated us,' he says. 'We could not cope.'

The demise of his beloved jazz festival remains one of his few regrets. Later he staged a folk festival. I remember hearing Julie Felix one year. It was fine. Perfectly enjoyable. No trouble. But it wasn't the same as the jazz festivals.

When I helped on *The Gilt and the Gingerbread*, Lord Montagu was already far and away the most professional and hard-headed stately home owner in the league. They were always called 'stately homes' in those days and it is one of Lord Montagu's many marketing triumphs to have succeeded in getting most of us to abandon that rather creaking, mildly pejorative description, in favour of the crisper, more acceptable term 'Historic House'. Perhaps I'm being unduly flattering in ascribing the change to him, but I do suspect that he has had more to do with it than anyone. No doubt it is something that we'll be told about one day by Philip Howard in *The Times*.

Even in the Sixties Lord Montagu and his increasingly professional team were more than capable of seeing off unwary management consultants who came sniffing around Beaulieu in the hope of turning a swift buck. Indeed, even then his advice was increasingly being sought by others who were being tempted to open their own houses for the first time or had done and got themselves into difficulties of one sort or another.

At the end of *The Gilt and the Gingerbread* there is an impassioned plea for more professionalism and more cohesion. As early as 1952 he and Sir Harold Wernher, the owner of Luton Hoo in Bedfordshire, tried to start what the press referred to as a 'trade union' of owners. It never caught on. Then, in 1965, the British Travel

Association set up a committee of owners including the most improbable one of the lot, the sometime Chairman of the Labour Party and compulsive homosexual, Tom Driberg. Montagu has always been a believer in that sort of concerted action by the owners. 'We must move with the times and act together before it is too late. We must remove the great prejudice against apparent wealth both at public and private levels.' Above all he was concerned that 'we must choose the right tools for the job, the tools of a professional.'

Twenty-five years on, Beaulieu itself is the acme of professionalism, and Montagu himself is a key player in a 'Heritage' game which has been transformed out of all recognition. The Historic Houses Association, of which he was the Founder President from 1973 to 1978, is now a power in the land, not perhaps exactly an owners' trade union but certainly an effective working alliance. And in 1983 Lord Montagu became Chairman of the Historic Buildings and Monuments Commission, or English Heritage as it is now known. The glossy modern incarnation of what used to be the stuffy old Department of Public Building and Works looks after four hundred sites open to the public.

It is by Beaulieu that he would wish to be judged. That original tiny collection of motor cars in the front hall of Palace House is now 'The National Motor Museum'; that eccentric Englishman's folly heralded in the national press under the headline 'Old crocks now on show at King John's Abbey' now consists of more than two hundred vehicles, not to mention thousands of documents, books, magazines and motoring ephemera housed in a special new building four times the size of its predecessor. It cost £2 million. Since 1970 the Museum has been a charitable trust, the deal being that Lord Montagu makes his collections available at a peppercorn rent for a minimum of sixty years.

On the day of the naming of the buffet car by Ralph Lord Montagu and I lunched alone. The private rooms seemed as cool, quiet and removed from the milling crowds as ever. The wine was from the Beaulieu vineyard and the fish from the Beaulieu river. Considering that we were at the nerve centre of one of the country's major tourist attractions, it seemed extraordinarily private. These rooms are all in the Victorian part of the house which was built for Lord Montagu's grandfather by Sir Arthur Blomfield, the architect of Selwyn College, Cambridge and the Queen's School at Eton.

The older rooms, those of the Abbey's Great Gatehouse, were made into a modest manor house after the Dissolution of the Monasteries, when Sir Thomas Wriothesley bought the eight thousand acre estate for £1,340 6s 8d. However, Palace House never had a resident owner until the Duke of Buccleuch gave it to his second son, Lord Henry Douglas-Scott-Montagu, as a wedding present in 1867. Blomfield made his additions in characteristic Victorian Gothick style. He approved the original buildings but not the eighteenth-century alterations, which he considered 'extremely defective'. Two wings at the north were completely demolished.

Despite new Blomfield and ancient monastery it is neither a big nor a grand house. Sensibly enough the style of presentation reflects this. Hugh Montgomery-Massingberd, who went there for his *Daily Telegraph* column in 1988, wrote approvingly of the 'vivid impression of country house life through the ages.' All the display material has been rewritten in the first person, so the style is much cosier and more intimate. Also agreeably jokey. In the kitchen display, for instance, we are told that Pleasant, the butler, 'wore a red Egyptian fez given to him by my grandfather', and that one of the more unusual jobs of the footmen 'was to scrub clean the small silver coins carried by the ladies'.

There's a pleasantly domestic character to many of the exhibits too. While 'Coronation Robes', for instance, have a chillingly formal ring to them, part of the Beaulieu Coronation Robe display is the black velvet suit the present Baron wore to George VI's coronation in 1937. He was the youngest peer present, a mere eleven years old. Alongside the suit is the bag in which he carried his ham sandwiches. It's difficult to think of a less stuffy Coronation Robe exhibit than the youngest peer's ham sandwich bag.

'My father . . . My wife Fiona . . . a family celebration on the occasion of my elder son's 21st birthday in 1982 . . . In 1907 Kaiser William II was entertained at Beaulieu by my father . . . My daughter Mary . . . My father pictured in India during the First World War where he was Inspector of Mechanical Transport for the Indian government . . . My youngest son Jonathan . . . A recent picture of me.'

It's the family album laid out for all to see: children in sailor suits, a wistful motorist in check cap, the Kaiser in a cloak and bowler hat with upturned waxed moustaches, Lord Montagu himself looking extraordinarily like his father only without the cap and the moustache. Elsewhere there are his grandfather's watercolours executed on a foreign holiday ordered by doctors who thought it would cure his asthma, photographs of gentlemen out shooting, the Gieves lifejacket which 'saved my father's life when the *SS Persia* was torpedoed in the First World War' and — reminding me of the newly named buffet car — the letter from the London South Western Railway to 'the Engineman' which says, 'Permit the bearer, the Hon. Scott Montagu and another to ride on the footplate of your Engine on Friday the 26th inst.' Lord Montagu adds a typically informative little aside: 'My father was a keen railway enthusiast, driving an engine during the General Strike of 1926.'

The effect of all this is to make you feel at home and involved, almost as if you are part of the family. You feel as if you had stumbled on an old photograph album in your own attic or come across a forgotten chest of drawers full of your own grandparents' knick-knacks. But do not be wholly deceived. Look again at the 'recent

picture of me'. It does not depict some corduroy-clad old buffer with a shotgun under his arm, it, shows a well-groomed chap in a suit, collar and tie sitting behind what looks like a tycoon-sized, red-topped desk. If you didn't know who it was you would, I think, guess that the man was the chairman of a company. And quite a large one. Public certainly, multi-national possibly. And should you, when you visit Beaulieu, catch a glimpse of this figure, watch him carefully for a second. See how his eyes dart hither and yon like the 'maître d' of a five-star restaurant. You may catch him stooping to pick up a scrap of paper, gently chiding a member of staff for some minor solecism, or simply greeting a member of the public.

At times Beaulieu may look quite effortlessly casual; but that sort of style is not achieved by chance. It is no accident, for instance, that Lord Montagu's Managing Director, Ken Robinson, is not only the most coveted in the stately home league but also, by common consent, the most amply rewarded. Twenty-five years ago, in *The Gilt and the Gingerbread*, Montagu wrote, 'Our ideals can be amateur but our methods must be professional.'

It should be the Montagu family motto.

MAUNSEL HOUSE

Sir Benjamin Slade was a school with me. Baronets were pretty thin on the ground at Connaught House School. It has closed now and been reincarnated as a health farm. There's a golf course in the park where they used to hold the gymkhana and Mr Hoyle, the headmaster, built the Guy Fawkes Night bonfire; jacuzzis instead of the communal footbath, designer salads instead of beans on toast. The house, Watt's House, just outside the Somerset village of Bishop's Lydeard, would have qualified for these pages if the Boles family – Somerset baronets like the Slades – hadn't moved out during the war.

In the 1950s, of course, Sir Benjamin Slade, Bart. was plain Slade, or Benjy to his friends. He was – and is – a year or two younger than me and a little older than my brother, now a respectable headmaster. My brother rather fell in with Benjy at one

stage and Mr Hoyle had to write a stiffish letter to my parents telling them that in his view the relationship should not be encouraged. I think he thought that Benjy would lead my brother astray.

One weekend my parents and my brother and I were invited to Maunsel, the Slades' house between Taunton and Bridgwater. I remember very little about the occasion except that the house was large and excessively dilapidated and obviously old. The family seemed to be beating a retreat against nature and decay and were holed up, if not in a single upstairs room, at least in one wing. It seemed a state of affairs unlikely to continue for much longer. Benjy's father, Sir Michael, was our host. My mother, who had been born and brought up at Martock, where the beans do come from, remembered Sir Michael as a rakish young man riding dashingly at the point-to-points of local hunts like the Quantock and the Taunton Vale. By the time of our drinks he had grown stout, and to me at twelve or so seemed bordering on old age. He must, I suppose, have been rather younger than I am now.

Our paths, as they say, diverged. Benjy went to Millfield and vanished into worlds of which I knew nothing. Much later I sighted him briefly at the curious Connaught House reunions we held in Taunton and once at the school itself. The small mischievous boy with the gingerish hair in the regulation blue Aertex shirt and navy shorts seemed to have been wearied by the years. Like his father he had grown stout and had an air of tailored double-breasted suit. His hair was prematurely grey.

This sense that Sir Benjamin had taken a battering from the storms of life was enhanced by a series of stories in *Private Eye*. Evidently our old schoolfriend now ran a container company called Shirlstar and one of his aeroplanes had been impounded by the Nigerian government. The plane appears still to be languishing on some West African runway. It was an incomprehensible story – at least to me – but the *Eye*, in its inimitably ghoulish way, managed to imply that poor Benjy had been up to no good and was about to come to no good too. I remembered Mr Hoyle's warning to my father.

Then, when I was starting out on this book, I was leafing through the pages of the *Historic Houses, Castles and Gardens* annual and came on an entry on page 152: Maunsel House, North Newton, nr. Bridgwater (Sir Benjamin Slade Bt.). I scanned it quickly. 'Ancestral seat of the Slade family under extensive restoration' . . . well it would have to be, wouldn't it . . . 'before Conquest' . . . 'Opening times, April 1 to Sept. 30' . . . 'Fishing, bring own tackle, £1. Boating, bring own boat, £1.' Boating, bring own boat! Really, Benjy! I decided to get in touch.

He seemed delighted to hear from me. 'How's your brother?' . . . 'Tell him to bring a school group from Street. We'll give them a reduced rate'. . . 'Come and stay the week-end.'

Much later he phoned. 'We're having a hunt ball. Not a very smart hunt ball. It's the Taunton Vale. No, black tie will be fine. Hardly anyone will be in tails. It's not that sort of hunt.'

So one Friday afternoon the illustrator and I took the train for Taunton with black ties in our bags, then drove to North Petherton where we took tea in the Best Westernized pub opposite the church and drove down winding lanes for a mile or so until just beyond the village of North Newton and before the Bridgwater and Taunton canal we came on the drive up to the house. It was impossible to miss because one front was almost wholly obscured by a huge marquee from Yeo Bros Paull of Martock.

The ensuing week-end was oddly surreal – part Wodehouse, a touch of Tom Sharpe, and for me a lot of straightforward nostalgia. I had last been to anything like this about a quarter of a century earlier, when, as an undergraduate, I occasionally and inappropriately found myself attempting the twist at Quaglino's or eating a 3 a.m. breakfast in a tent in the Cotswolds. At first there was no sign of our host, just Lady Slade and a friend from Northamptonshire taking tea in the upstairs drawing-room. We introduced ourselves slightly nervously and then Sir Benjamin arrived, hail fellow well met, fined down a little, carrying a hunting horn and wearing a hat in the form of an elk's head. He had already warned me that the house was still under-plumbed, following years of neglect, and in any case likely to be full of house party. He thought we'd be better off in the Best Westernized pub in North Petherton so had, accordingly billeted us there.

We drank tea while Sir Benjamin showed us some videos of the house and its owners, shot by local TV companies, and some newspaper cuttings. The owner emerged from these as a character with a capital C. 'Character' was also clearly what the house had in abundance. As various house guests made their entrances like so many characters in a William Douglas-Home play, Sir Benjamin told us a little about his Aunt Freda. 'She did for my family what Dutch elm disease did for the country-side,' he said, with feeling. 'Freda the Bleeder. Lived off Mars Bars and whisky. She drank for Somerset.' Also a Character, clearly. After selling most of the estate the Slades retained the right to ride along the banks of the Bridgwater and Taunton canal. The local anglers didn't care for this idea and took to laying their bicycles across the towpath. Aunt Freda was undeterred and treated the obstacles as if they were steeplechase fences. She would gallop over the bicycles, exercising her ancient feudal rights while crying out loud, 'I'm a Slade! I'm a Slade!'

On our return from bathing and changing in North Petherton we found the atmosphere transformed. On the stairs, the smooth gentleman immediately in front of me turned out to have been an Oxford contemporary. We swapped reminiscence. In the drawing-room, where the noise level had risen in tune with the alcohol consumption, Sir Benjamin had changed into a dinner jacket but retained the hunting

horn and the elkhorn hat. The obvious farming chap with the ruddy outdoor complexion was the middle of the three Stoddarts who had all been at Connaught House with me and lived at Cothelstone, half-way up the Quantocks. The sharp good-looking woman addressed by Sir Benjamin simply as 'Wilcox' turned out to be the Chairman of the National Consumer Council, Lady Wilcox. She was incredibly knowledgeable and entertaining about, of all things, the fishing industry. The chap who looked like a Household Cavalry major was a painter and the pretty blonde was his sister, Sophie, who worked in Pictures and Prints at Holland & Holland.

And so on. Downstairs in the tent the rest of the country bopped away to the sound of Mike D'Abo, a name which either made one feel old or reassured, because, surely, he had once sung with Manfred Mann and been a feature at Commem Balls in the Sixties. Or was that another Mike D'Abo? Perhaps this was his son Mike D'Abo Two. The illustrator and I made our excuses quite early and ended up in the bar of our hotel chatting to the landlord and his wife about the peculiarities of the people up at the big house.

The rest of the weekend continued in predictable vein, with a mildly hung-over Saturday giving way to a sit-down Sunday lunch with more school-friends not seen these thirty years and more (one of whom accused me of dying my hair) and the owners of practically every historic house in the whole of the south-west. It was all very jolly and noisy and inbred, seasoned with a set of assumptions and prejudices scarcely credible among the sort of professional metropolitan chatterers with whom I normally mix and who are responsible for shaping what is laughably thought to be 'public opinion'.

To all of this the house was an entirely appropriate if shambolic background. To say that it had suffered years of neglect was a manifest understatement. Essentially the story was that Uncle Alfred and Aunt Freda ran the place into the ground. When Uncle Alfred died in 1960, Sir Benjamin's father Michael inherited, only to die a few months later, leaving Aunt Freda in possession. She stayed on as a sitting tenant, paying a pound a year until she died in 1982. 'It took me twenty years to sort out the mess,' he says. 'There were cockerels in the bloody loo. And when I took over I had to start with just a third of an acre.'

Despite an impressive amount of refurbishment the house still has a wonderfully higgledy-piggledy air. You feel that ever since Domesday in 1086, when a kinsman of the Conqueror's named Count Eustace of Boulogne was in charge, every single owner was determined to add something – a gargoyle, a flying buttress, a cupola, a weather-vane (I counted five weather-vanes), so the house is like a living scrapbook of English domestic architecture through the ages.

In Henry II's reign William de Erleigh granted Maunsel to someone called Philip Arbalistarius as a dowry to his daughter Mabel. In return he was to receive two pigs

every Whitsun. Arbalistarius's son Philip married the daughter of Sir Hugh d'Aud-
erville and, in a sensible move, changed his name to Maunsel. This was later corrupt-
ed to Mansel. The name derives from the old French for 'sleeve of land', presumably
coming from the same root as 'manche', meaning sleeve of water or English channel.
In due course the estate passed to the Bacon family of Norfolk and from them, in the
mid eighteenth century, to the Slades themselves.

If the fabric of the house is a disaster the parkland is, if anything, even worse.
The baronet is buying it back – on borrowed money. But it's not just that the land
itself has been sold. During the war hundreds of ancient trees were felled for timber
and there's no denying that the park today has a sadly naked look. The morning after
the dance, however, Sir Benjamin was walking his lawns with a restorative mug of tea
and waving his other arm with the enthusiasm of a latter-day Capability Brown. 'I
hate that hedge,' he said, pointing at a harmless line of bush. 'So that's going. And I'm
going to plant a walnut avenue there. And there.' He is devoted to walnuts, not just
because they are fine and beautiful trees but because they make economic sense as
well. They'll take years to achieve maturity, but when they do the yield per acre will
be greater than anything comparable. Beauty and profit, hand in hand. 'And there'll
be a lake there,' he says, with another lordly gesture. He has a fleet of terrifying heavy
earth-moving vehicles which tear about the estate and have already excavated an
ornamental pond to the immediate south of the house. It is home to no fewer than
thirty-six different variety of birds, mostly imported by his wife from Slimbridge, the
National Wildfowl Trust reserve in Gloucestershire.

It would have been much easier to sell up and stay in London, but as so often
with these family homes, the old ghosts have the last word. Away beyond the lawn
and Mill Cottage where he lived in Aunt Freda's day there is the tiny church of St
Michael, next to the field where the farm manager accidentally shot himself in 1944.
There the Slades lie buried, including his father Sir Michael. We were conducted
there by Frank, the man about Maunsel of whom Sir Benjamin says, with mock exas-
peration, 'I'm always trying to pay him off but he never goes.' It's a sad, forlorn rest-
ing-place for the Slades. And although he never says anything so romantic or
sentimental, the last of the Slades cannot betray their memory.

And so he struggles on.

I hope the old schoolfriend makes it, because it was good to see his ancestral
home come alive that week-end. Maybe it is only bricks and mortar but after a while
you begin to feel these houses have a soul and they were meant to reverberate to the
sound of music and talk of hunting and shooting and the pop of corks. Far better
have a hunt ball at Maunsel than at some tacky modern hotel. It's a house that is
meant to be full of people having a good time.

Besides, his attitude is right. As we walked the grounds he gestured away

towards some distant flatness and said 'Wetlands'. Pause. 'Good for snipe shooting. The SSI people say they're good for butterflies.' Pause again. 'They also said that a hole in the ground they found was an ancient Roman claypit, but actually it was where the Germans dropped a bomb in the last war.' He laughs a short, disrespectful laugh which reminds me briefly of the cheeky boy at school.

The paying public are, of course, part of the plans, and his attitude towards them is as robust as his attitude towards authority and the experts, even if it's more friendly. 'The public,' he says, 'like things they can identify with. They don't identify with Rembrandts or Canalettos. They like to look at the wiring.'

It is abundantly clear that the public are not, at least while Sir Benjamin Slade has anything to do with it, going to get any Rembrandts or Canalettos at Maunsel. But there will be plenty of wiring, some of it ancient and exposed.

At least for the time being.

MIDELNEY MANOR

The Taunton Vale Hunt Ball at Maunsel was in full swing when suddenly a faintly florid figure in tails and white tie entered Sir Benjamin and Lady Slade's drawing-room and called out, in the style of a no-nonsense, horse-whipping country squire in the Henry Fielding/Tobias Smollet mould, 'Which one is Tim Heald?' Had he then slapped his thigh and cried 'Gadzooks!' or drawn a sword and exclaimed, 'Damn my heart and liver, you dog!' I should not have been altogether surprised. He had that sort of manner and appearance, especially in a tailcoat.

I should have replied, 'Odds Niggers! You must be Squire John Cely Trevilian of Midelney! Good Morrow, sirrah.'

Alas, I lacked the spirit and instead said something along the lines of 'Er, me, actually.'

We shook hands. I had first written to him months before and he had replied civilly, asked me to a falcon flying display in August when, unfortunately, I was away. He had also enclosed a reprint of an old *Country Life* article with the not altogether unjustified comment: 'Should give you a background to the place if you can get to the end of it without falling asleep.' Because he lived in the sort of house he did, and in the same county as Sir Benjamin Slade I had guessed he might well be at the Ball. He might not be a baronet, but his is an old family. The first Trevilian was said to be the only man to escape from Lyonesse. A nice piece of Arthurian legend.

It was too late to talk architecture or genealogy, so our conversation turned to the more pressing matter of the following day's rugby international. Like me, Trevilian was a rugger enthusiast, although because he had lived for some years north of the border his loyalties seemed dangerously divided. Anyway, he invited me and the illustrator over for lunch next day. Afterwards we would watch the rugger and he'd give me the guided tour.

The drive from North Newton to Midelney was across county. At least we chose to make it across country and inevitably got lost in the middle of that slightly spooky canal-cut flatness near Glastonbury. Finally we made it to Curry Rivel, from which there were signs to the Manor. It lies at the end of a road that peters out into nothing just beyond the house.

The Trevilian standard, white horses on black, white stars on blue, a gold chevron and various other heraldic complexities, was flying from a mast to the right immediately above some immaculate topiary hedge. The house to the left was exquisite, a low U of light honey stone which I presumed was quarried from Ham Hill, not far away just above Montacute. Quite small – no more really than a beautiful farmhouse.

It was very quiet, and naturally every door was open. We tried a nervous knock and a tentative 'Hello!' Nothing. Perhaps the Trevilians were still sleeping off the night before. We tiptoed in and suddenly found ourselves straight through the house and into an *Alice in Wonderland* garden – a series of quadrangles like a rural Oxford college leading to woodlands at the far end. We wandered up the path, listening to the caw of rooks, turned and came back. It was so peaceful that we began to think the house was some sort of *Marie Celeste*, adrift in this sylvan paradise above Sedge-moor. And then, greatly daring, we pushed a door open and found a small group of ladies round a dining-room table quietly drinking champagne. They were as surprised to see us as we were to see them, but when we explained all became clear. It was all part of English country life. Invitations issued in the middle of Hunt Balls tend to be forgotten as the revels progress. It is also customary at a week-end morning for the man of the house to take his male friends to the local pub, leaving the ladies to prepare lunch. This was what had happened. Squire Trevilian and his cronies were down at the local hostelry quaffing ale, while their ladies attended the domestic chores as befitted their station. Odds Bodkins! Fielding and Smollett would have approved – though they *were* drinking champagne.

Anyway we were made very welcome and given champagne, and presently the gentlemen returned. John Trevilian was overcome with remorse and rendered the most abject apologies. Then we all sat down to delicious bangers and mash and later went off to the drawing-room to watch the rugby on television.

The facts about the house are mostly either sketchy or plain. The writer of the seminal, if soporific, 1934 *Country Life* article says at one point that 'the house has been so much altered that it is impossible to be certain about dates.' Alongside this uncertainty is the incontrovertible evidence of family tree and family portrait that the Trevilians, while salt of the earth, backbone of England and all round sound fellows, are not the sort of people who grab headlines. Like so many other estates that we looked at, it was originally a religious property that was privatized when Henry VIII dissolved the monasteries in the 1530s. The consequences of that single act on the pattern of rural life in England were phenomenal.

Midelney was originally an island, the road from Curry Rivel a causeway. If you wanted to get from Midelney to its larger more prosperous neighbour, Muchelney, you had to get a boat. Muchelney Abbey's first charter, which dates from around AD 700, records a grant from King Ina of the West Saxons. This specifies Midelney as the 'middle island' between 'the great island' (Muchelney) and 'the isle of thorns' (Thorney).

In the Middle Ages the Muchelney Abbots used Midelney as a place for summer holidays. They kept a pack of hounds and created a deer park. In the early fourteenth century the Abbot let the land to an interesting parvenu called Ralph of Midelney who, though successful as a soldier, was in frequent trouble for 'turbulence'. He sounds like a medieval Kray and was once sent on a pilgrimage to Santiago de Compostella for his sins. His descendants, whose arms, curiously and unappealingly consisted of 'three snayles', continued to rent the land from the Abbots till the Dissolution. The King then made the Manor over to the Earl of Hertford, later Protector Somerset, who in turn made it over to a John Trevilian of Kingsbury. In 1603 his grandson finally bought it and it has remained in the family ever since.

Despite the *Country Life* uncertainties over dates, it seems that the core of the house was constructed by the two sons of John Trevilian, Richard and Thomas. The oddity is that, although they shared the house, they did not get on and built it in two separate self-contained sections. The theory is that Richard, the elder, who lived in the west half, married beneath him, while Thomas married appropriately. His wife

was a Jennings of Burton Pynsent, later to be Pitt the Elder's house. His nephew Ralph also married a Jennings of Burton, and so did Ralph's grandson.

In the eighteenth century John Trevilian, High Sheriff of Somerset, decided to make the house (or houses) grander. To do this he reversed it, making the back door the front and the main approach through the deer park. He also knocked down the north wings and built a mews for falcons.

John died without children and the house went to his sister Mellicent, who married a William Ceely of Charlton. Their son, William, one of ten, took the Trevilian name but had no money. The house began to disintegrate, though William still maintained the family pack of hounds, a legacy from the days of the Abbots. In 1781 his nephew John abandoned the house and it was let as a farm; the hounds were sold and the deer park was ploughed up. Not until 1926 did Major M. F. Cely Trevilian decide to move the family back to its old home and set it in order.

It now seems to be in exceedingly good nick. The general air of 'peace and happiness' which the *Country Life* writer noticed more than fifty years ago was still much in evidence. John Cely Trevilian was a generous host and his guests were extremely relaxed. There was a lot of sprawling around chatting in a house which seemed designed for just that. Indeed the Trevilians are turning this atmosphere to commercial effect by offering the house as an unusual sort of small conference centre. 'An exclusive setting for corporate hospitality and entertaining, for special meetings and private discussions,' says their brochure. 'You will find in us an ideal venue for small seminars and company conferences, as well as discreet product-launches.' Much better than 'even the best of hotels', which are lambasted as 'staid and stuffy'.

There's nothing staid or stuffy about the Trevilians of Midelney. Even less so, I should think, if John gets his apple brandy project off the ground, though we won't know about this for a year or so. Of all the houses I saw on these travels, Midelney is probably the least pretentious but in many ways it is the one I most covet. It reminds me of a line in *Peregrine Pickle*: 'All your care is to sit among your companions of the garden and sing bunting-songs till you get drunk.' Midelney is just the place for drinking and singing bunting-songs in the garden, and if I were organizing a modest sales conference I should hire it at once.

STRATFIELD SAYE HOUSE

Poor Duke! The victor of Waterloo, most indomitable of Britain's military heroes – the one thing he dreaded was Queen Victoria paying him a visit at Stratfield Saye, the Berkshire house which he had purchased with the £600,000 voted to him by a grateful nation after his victory in 1815.

'Alas!' he wrote to Lady Wilton, in December 1844. 'It is but too true: the Queen is coming to pay me a visit at Stratfield Saye. I did everything I could to avoid the Subject: never mentioned the word Stratfield Saye, and kept out of Her Way. But . . .'

Summoned to Windsor for a meeting of the Order of the Bath, he was unable to avoid the Queen, who very charmingly invited herself to stay. The old man was beside himself.

'The Difficulty under which I labour, besides the Numbers to be received in comparatively a small House, consists in my having no State apartment. H.M. and H.M. Court requiring a sitting Room as well as the usual Lodging Rooms and best Rooms for their attendants, not few in Number, with Bells ringing into the same from H.M. Apartments. Bells must be hung from H.M. Apartments into those for Her Attendants, Walls broken through, &c. You recollect poor Mrs. Apostles the Housekeeper. I thought that she would have burst out crying while I was talking to Her of the Honour intended and the preparations to be made. She said to me, very nearly in the Words which I had used two nights before to H.M., "My Lord, Your House is a very comfortable residence for yourself, your Family and your friends; But it is not fit for the Reception of the Sovereign and Her Court." I answered, "Very True! But H.M.'s coming is decided; what cannot be prevented must be borne; and we must make the best preparation in our Power." '

It all turned out for the best. In her diary, the Queen wrote: 'Stratfieldsaye [sic] is a low & not very large house, but warm & comfortable & with a great deal of room in it. We arrived at 5. The good old Duke received us at the door . . . The Duke took us into the Library, a nice long room & then, to our own rooms. We have a nice little sitting room & then along a small passage, our bedroom, a snug room, opening into my small dressing room & Albert also has a dressing room.'

This sounds like enough rooms, and most of them 'nice'. The Duke came personally and fetched them for Dinner, sat on the sofa next to the Queen, helped them personally at luncheon – 'rather funnily, giving such large portions & mixing up tarts & puddings together, but he is so kind & attentive about it'. The Duke even saw them to bed. 'The Duke has each evening walked upstairs before me with a candle.' After Albert had composed a duet which the Royal couple sang they went to the Tennis Court, where the Duke's marker and the Duke's butler, 'a fat man called Philips who plays beautifully', put on a demonstration. Finally they set off just as they came, with 'the good old Duke riding before us'.

As soon as she had gone the Duke sat down and wrote to Lady Wilton. 'I thank God!' he wrote, 'The visitation is concluded. I have just now returned from attending Her Majesty on Horseback to the Borders of the County.

'I hope that H.M. has been as well pleased as I have been with all that has passed. She was in perfect good Humour during the whole Time, very gracious to everybody; and everybody pleased.'

A good visit in the end, though by the standards of Blenheim, which is the obvious comparison, Stratfield Saye is indeed a modest house. That is not because the first Duke of Wellington was much less given to ostentation than the first Duke of Marlborough. When he was looking for a suitable house in 1817, Wellington considered several which were far grander, including Bramshill (now the Police College) and Uppark, which was gutted in the infamous fire of 1989. In the end he opted for Stratfield Saye, built in about 1630 by Sir William Pitt, Comptroller of the Household to James I. But he actually bought it with the intention of knocking it down and building another Blenheim.

No house I know is so absolutely redolent of a single man, particularly one who has been dead for almost a hundred and fifty years, His descendant, the 8th Duke, tells the story of John Fowler, the interior decorator, who remarked after walking round the house, 'I feel the Great Duke only left here twenty-five years ago.' Reminded of this a year or two later he said, 'Twenty-five years ago? I meant five.'

'I think you will feel the same,' says the present Duke with evident approval.

The illustrator and I approached the house on foot from one of the lodge gates, our taxi driver having been unable to find a way in. As a result we were late, and as we arrived the Duke and a labrador were just getting into a Range Rover on their way to see a man about a tree. The latest round of storms had hit Stratfield Saye distressingly hard. The country's largest liquid amber was down. So were a number of the estate's eponymous Wellingtonias. I'd heard that the Duke could be a little brisk on occasion, which is one reason that I'd approached him through the good offices of his daughter, the film-maker Jane Wellesley, a former hackette with whom I'd once worked happily on the *Radio Times*. There was just a moment when I thought the present Duke was going to react rather as the first Duke when confronted by a group of mutinous Army doctors. 'I accept your resignations and I shall immediately write home for a fresh Medical Staff. But, mark me, until they come out you shall remain here and you shall perform your duties.'

But he didn't.

'My father came here in 1944 after my aunt moved out in '43,' he explained a little later over a glass of sherry, in glasses with an etching of that unmistakeable ducal profile on the side. 'At that time it was incredibly primitive. No electric light or heating. I was abroad on active service, but when I came home on leave we used to sit around a Tilly lamp. All the ceilings were black from the oil lamps and we went to bed with candles just like they did when Queen Victoria came to stay.'

We were sitting in the Lady Charles room, which was restored and redecorated by John Fowler in 1973. This Duke succeeded in 1972, so the restoration was almost the first thing he did. It's a light, very lived in small drawing-room, the heart of the family corner of the house. 'All the things here,' he said, 'belonged to my grandfather, the fourth Duke. That's him,' he gestured to a family group by Gambardella facing the window, 'holding the dog's paw.'

The Duke talks you round that room as if it were an ordinary man's photo album. It's called the Lady Charles Room after Augusta Sophia Pierrepont who married Lord Charles Wellesley, second son of the Great Duke. She presides over the family portrait by Gambardella which not only includes Arthur, the present Duke's grandfather, but also his sister Victoria and Henry, the third Duke. Lady Charles, who died in 1893, is the Wellesley Materfamilias. All but the first two dukes are descended from her.

'She was descended from the Dukes of Kingston,' said the Duke (I was going to distinguish him from his predecessors by calling him Arthur, but then realized that he is the fifth Duke to be so called). The Duke raised his eyebrows and told me about the famous Duchess of Kingston who married a Bristol and precipitated a celebrated bigamy trial in the House of Lords. This is tactfully omitted from the official guide-book. Not so 'Rough', 'Gruff' and 'Elegant Stuff'. 'Elegant Stuff' was Lady Charles's father Henry and 'Rough' and 'Gruff' were his brothers. Their (small) portraits hang between the doors. 'Now that horse there over the door,' the Duke pointed again, 'was Henry Pierrepont's. It belonged to Marshal Berthier who was one of Napoleon's generals. It was on the retreat from Moscow.' Berthier died in 1815 shortly before Waterloo. Pierrepont bought the horse in Paris, named it Moscow and brought it home. 'It's a Landseer,' said the Duke. 'His very first commission. He was sixteen years old when he did that.' An extra oddity is that the picture was stolen before it could be delivered. It was discovered twenty-four years later in 1842 in a loft over Landseer's stables, where it had apparently been secreted by one of his grooms.

Landseer, by then the celebrated Sir Edwin, delivered it to Pierrepont with an invoice for the same amount that he would have charged as a sixteen-year-old: ten guineas.

The pictures are not Wellingtonia in the Grand Ducal sense but continue the Caroline theme: a Kneller of her grandfather the first Duke of Kingston, several paintings of her great-grandfather with various horses (one showing him trying to teach the future George III to ride), two of her mother Sophie Cecil (who died at 23), and one of her maternal grandfather the first Marquess of Exeter who married Sara Hoggins, daughter of the village blacksmith. Tennyson wrote a poem about the match, and jolly melancholy it is too. When Miss Hoggins met Lord Burleigh (sic) she thought he was a mere landscape painter. When she discovered that 'Not a lord in all the county/Is so great a lord as he', she married him none the less, but the burden of 'an honour unto which she was not born' proved too much.

> So she droop'd and droop'd before him,
> Fading slowly from his side.
> Three fair children first she bore him,
> Then before her time she died.

Everywhere else at Stratfield Saye you feel as if the Great Duke is about to come out from behind a pillar and say something that will make you curl up and die. This is unfair, because he was not really a curmudgeon. Indeed, even in his day he let the public in. His original admonition is still on display:

'Those desirous of seeing the interior of the House are requested to ring at the door of entrance and to express their desire. It is wished that the practice of stopping on the paved walk to look in at the windows should be discontinued.'

His great-great-grandson, when asked about opening to the public, catches an echo of this. 'Well,' he says, 'it can be a bit of a bore sometimes.'

Some of the Great Duke's improvements are still in evidence. Two of the vast radiators he installed are still in working order and were recently connected to a new heating system. He also put in blue and white china water-closets. The two outer wings were added in 1846 and he also built on a conservatory in 1838. This now houses an elegant swimming pool and some great marble pillars which he imported from Italy in 1821. These are a sad reminder of his unfulfilled ambition to build a really splendid 'Waterloo Palace'. They were intended to be part of this ambitious project, but his £600,000 wouldn't stretch to it (Look at Benjamin Wyatt's architectural drawings and plans in 'the corridor' and you'll see why. The palace would have been ginormous.) The Italian columns weren't even unpacked until 1947, when the 7th Duke decided they would be just the thing for the pool.

One reason for the preservation of the original interior is that for much of the first part of this century the house was unoccupied. 'They just turned the key and walked out,' says the present Duke. When they came back during the Second World War it was just as it had been before the First, bar the dust. Not only the marble pillars were in their original wrapping. Loads of the great Duke's clothes and poss-essions were still in trunks and cases, almost as if he too might come back one day and reclaim his property.

It's the little things that I always find most affecting: The old man's magnifying glass and telescope, the bottles of rosewater for his failing eyes, the bracelet that Queen Victoria always wore (it contained a lock of the Great Duke's hair). And the strange little traditions. In the entrance hall, for instance, are the Napoleonic banners given as tribute when the Duke entered Paris after Waterloo. I'd half expected them, but what I wasn't prepared for were the small tricolour flags at each end. These are samples of the flags which are presented to the Sovereign by the Duke at an annual ceremony (usually dinner at Windsor Castle) on or before Waterloo Day on 18 June. They're the symbolic peppercorn rent to the Crown.

We had walked in from the east through the stable block. Although it made us late it's the best way to approach the house, because the effect of the stables on both sides of the drive is to make the house look much more imposing than it really is. The stables now house a Wellington museum, choc-a-bloc with every conceivable item of clothing, including, irresistibly, the first ever pair of Wellington boots. The stables also contain the Duke's incredible hearse or 'Funeral Car', as it was described in 1852, the year of his death. You might have guessed that its design was personally supervised by Prince Albert himself. It weighs eighteen tons, its six wheels are made of bronze cast from melted-down French cannons captured at Waterloo. Above the base is a swivelling platform to enable the coffin to be slid on to a special ramp over the steps of St Paul's cathedral. All the Duke's victories are recorded in gold and there is a ferocious display of cuirasses, helmets, spears, colours and standards. The velvet pall was embroidered with the Wellesley crest and there was even a halberd-support-ed canopy on top to keep the rain off. Too much, of course. It could only just squeeze under Temple Bar, which had a clearance of seventeen feet, and it twice got stuck, in the Mall and on Ludgate Hill. The swivel platform didn't work properly either, with the result that on a very inclement day the Cathedral doors had to be kept open for an hour-and-a-half. This monstrous thing is far too ornate for the Duke, but it is still magnificent. After a brief stay in a shed at Marlborough House it went to the crypt of St Paul's, where it remained till 1981, when it was brought home to Stratfield Saye.

A more romantic piece of funereal history is the cypress in the Pleasure Gardens. After the funeral a sprig of cypress was plucked from one of the wreaths on the 'Car'. This took root and grew into a tree. In 1953, Lady Jane, the Duke's great-great-great-granddaughter planted a cutting from that tree in the Pleasure Grounds and that too has become a tall cypress. I feel the Duke would have liked that.

The Pleasure Grounds that day were, alas, not looking up to their name. The sec-ond of the great storms had cut a terrible swathe through them and scores of massive trees had fallen and were lying, dead, beside vast craters where their roots had been. Many of these trees were planted by Wellington himself. Indeed there is a plaque in the park commemorating the planting of a cedar of Lebanon by him on his very first visit in September 1817. Just as inside the house, his mark is everywhere. There is even a noble tombstone which reads: 'Here Lies Copenhagen, the Charger Ridden by the Duke of Wellington the entire day at the battle of Waterloo. Born 1808. Died 1830.' In retirement the old horse was ridden by the Duke and his children. 'God's humbler instrument, though meaner clay,' continues the inscription, 'Should share the glory of that glorious day.' The more I get to know the Duke the more I like him.

The Wellingtonias, which I had vaguely supposed to have been planted by him, were in fact introduced only in 1853, a year after his death, but many of the other trees must have been his. So were the elaborate gardens, now fully restored after years of neglect, though the Real Tennis court where the marker and the fat butler entertained the Queen and Albert has been pulled down and only the outline remains.

Sad, but not as sad as all those fallen trees. My abiding memory of Stratfield Saye is of coming across the Duchess, standing surveying the desolation. When I commiserated, her response would have done credit to the Great Duke himself.

'Oh well,' she said with the sort of Blitz common sense which the British like to think is peculiar to them, 'you just have to clear up and plant again for someone else to enjoy.'

CASTLE HOWARD

S uddenly a new and secret landscape opened before us. We were at the head of a valley and below us, half a mile distant, grey and gold amid a screen of boskage, shone the dome and columns of an old house.'
This, you will recall, is Charles Ryder's first glimpse of the Castle in *Brideshead Revisited*, and because of the hugely successful television series based on Evelyn Waugh's book many of those who visit Castle Howard in Yorkshire do actually believe that it is the ancestral home of Lord and Lady Marchmain. They half expect Jeremy Irons and Anthony Andrews to come lolloping along the corridor in white flannels, they feel certain that nanny is lurking in an attic and Laurence Olivier receiving the last sacraments in bed upstairs, even though they know from their glossy brochure that the reality is quite otherwise. 'We'll never get away from Brideshead,' concedes the Hon. Simon Howard, whose family first built this fabulous domed palace and who have lived here ever since. He smiles and shrugs. It *is* inescapable. For all who watched the TV series Castle Howard *is* Brideshead. Mind you, in an earlier celluloid incarnation, in the 1966 Galton and Simpson farce, *The Spy with the Cold Nose*, the house doubled for the Kremlin. It was supposed to look like it – at least under cover of darkness.

In 1944, when Waugh wrote his book, it seemed to him 'that the ancestral seats which were our chief national artistic achievement were doomed to decay and spoliation like the monasteries in the sixteenth century.'

Wrong, and wrong even in Waugh's own lifetime. As early as 1959, writing from his own country mansion at Combe Florey in Somerset – very much *not* open to the public – he conceded that the English aristocracy had hung on rather better than he had anticipated and that 'Brideshead today would be open to trippers, its treasures rearranged by expert hands and the fabric better maintained than it was by Lord Marchmain.'

In real life, Castle Howard today does indeed attract paying visitors – the management would never be caught using a word like 'tripper'. Over 200,000 people come every year and the enterprise is professionally organized under the auspices of a company called Castle Howard Estates Limited, which has three Howard brothers on its board. Its successful survival is by no means unique and Waugh's pessimism

turned out to be so unwarranted that his book was, as he later conceded, 'a panegyric preached over an empty coffin'. The stately homes of England may not be quite what they were, but they have, on the whole, survived with style.

Castle Howard is a gloriously unexpected place to find in the tough, wild landscape of North Yorkshire, its gilded dome towering over formal gardens and distant lakes, the famous Hawksmoor mausoleum dominating a field of sheep. Walpole wrote of this that it 'would tempt one to be buried alive'. This is carrying things too far. Not even a last resting place designed by Nicholas Hawksmoor could have quite such a seductive quality. The mausoleum is too spooky to beckon, gauntly protected by a covey of dark birds wheeling around its cupola, but it undoubtedly has an immense melancholy which I couldn't help feeling was rather wasted on the sheep or the occasional low flying military aircraft blasting home after the Gulf War.

The public have been admitted ever since the house's original construction in the early eighteenth century. In 1829 a visitor remarked that 'the liberality of the noble proprietor in admitting the public to view the contents of this elegant repository entitles him to grateful applause.' An inn – latterly a temperance inn – was even built to accommodate the curious, and before the last war the house was open three days a week with the admission fees going to charity. When, in 1966, I asked Simon Howard's father the late George what he felt about the loss of privacy involved in opening, he replied that he didn't mind because 'I have been used to it all my life.'

On the approaches to Castle Howard there is a hundred-foot obelisk, where, under six lines of rhyming couplets explaining the purpose of 'this faithful pillar', there is a simple statement that 'Charles the III Earl of Carlisle of the family of the Howards erected a castle where the old castle of Henderskelfe stood and called it Castle-Howard. He likewise made the plantations in this park and all the outworks, monuments and other plantations belonging to the said seat. He began these works in the year MDCCII ANNO D:MDCCXXXI.'

There is, naturally, rather more to it than that, and the story of the conception and construction could and has taken volumes to tell. The Castle Howard branch of the Howard family began with Lord William Howard, the son of the Duke of Norfolk who had his head cut off in 1572 for trying to marry Mary Queen of Scots. Lord William, known as 'Belted Will' and, by Sir Walter Scott, as 'The Civiliser of Our Borders' inherited the Henderskelfe estate by marrying Elizabeth Dacre, the daughter of his father's third wife by an earlier marriage – all very dynastically grasping.

It was his great-grandson who was made 1st Earl of Carlisle by Charles II after an astonishing series of volte-faces during the Civil War years. His grandson, the 3rd Earl, became a man of immense public influence, with a chain of offices ranging from Earl Marshal and First Lord of the Treasury to Lord Lieutenant of the Tower Hamlets. In 1693 Henderskelfe Castle was badly damaged by fire and the Earl decided that a new palace should be built in its place so as to demonstrate his eminence and importance. To carry this out he appointed Sir John Vanbrugh, a fellow member of the Kit Cat Club and author of the celebrated comedies *The Relapse* and *The Provok'd Wife*. This was a curious choice as Vanbrugh had never designed a building in his life. He was, however, an imaginative genius, and with the technically brilliant Nicholas Hawksmoor as his lieutenant, Castle Howard was always going to be a success. When the 3rd Earl wrote his will he commended 'Sir John Vanbrugh and Nicholas Hawksmoor with whose performance I am very well satisfied'. He lies now in the mausoleum.

The 4th Earl spent many years in Rome, amassing a collection of busts and statues, much of which is still in the castle, but also allowing his brother-in-law, Sir Thomas Robinson, to complete the house with a Palladian west wing which had nothing to do with Vanbrugh's original plans. His successor the 5th Earl was moved to comment: 'One of the things most difficult for any of us to comprehend was my father's building of the new wing at Castle Howard. Sir Thomas Robinson, whom he laughed at, by perpetual teasing carried his point, and my father gave way when his faculties had no appearance of being weakened. He lived long enough to be disgusted with all its uncomparable faults.'

For all his censoriousness the 5th Earl, who succeeded at the age of ten, was not an unqualified success himself, acquiring expensive tastes on the Grand Tour with Charles James Fox. He was Lord North's Chief Commissioner to North America and later Lord Lieutenant of Ireland, from which job he was sacked by Rockingham in 1782. He did, however, contribute some priceless Italian paintings to the Castle Howard collection.

The 6th and 7th Earls were both Members of Parliament before moving to the Upper House, both held high office, and both became Knights of the Garter. The 7th Earl, who wrote poetry and whose portrait shows him wearing a rather wonderful wide-brimmed white hat with a feather, never married and was succeeded by his brother, for more than forty years Rector of Londesborough but a victim, in later life, of 'mental infirmity'. Because of this the house was occupied by another brother, Admiral Edward Howard, until a nephew, George, painter, Pre-Raphaelite friend of Morris and Burne-Jones, became the 9th Earl.

In 1921, when Rosalind, Countess of Carlisle, died, the family estates were dived and Castle Howard went to the Hon. Geoffrey Howard, Liberal MP and Parliamentary Private Secretary to Asquith when Prime Minister. On his death in 1935 the house passed to family trustees. Two of his sons were killed in the last war – one in Normandy and one with the Dam Busters – but a third son, Major George, survived and came home to discover that a bad fire in November 1940 had destroyed the dome and two-thirds of the south front. The house, which had been occupied by a

girls' school, was now empty, and the trustees were selling off the contents on the grounds that no one would be foolish enough to attempt to live at Castle Howard ever again.

George Howard thought otherwise. Somehow he managed to combine the restoration of Castle Howard, including the rebuilding of the dome, with a public career worthy of his ancestors. Though such jobs as Lord Lieutenant of Ireland and Chief Commissioner of Woods and Forests were no longer available, he was a notable Chairman of the Governors of the BBC. His son, Simon, who worked as his deputy at the house until his death in 1984, says that it was only possible because he was such a formidable workaholic. As soon as he came home to Yorkshire at the week-end he would throw himself wholly into affairs of estate.

The illustrator and I came to Castle Howard on a quiet damp day in March about a fortnight before they were due to open for the 1991 season and, as usual, there were repairs taking place. This time it was the organ in the ornate Pre-Raphaelite chapel with its William Morris – Burne-Jones stained glass. There were pipes everywhere and one couldn't help wondering if the repairers would ever be able to fit them all together again, let alone in such a way that they could play a tune. The chapel, of course, features prominently in *Brideshead* as the focus of Marchmain Roman Catholicism, but in real life has always been Anglican, ever since it was installed in the 1870s. The organ originally cost £835.10s. In the recent severe frosts one of the ancient radiators had split and a new one was being installed, together with a covering to conceal its modernity. Vanbrugh would have been peeved about this, for during a cold snap in 1713 he once wrote, 'Though we have now had as bitter storms as rain and wind can well compose, every room in the House is like an oven and in corridors of 200 foot long there is not air enough to stir the flame of a candle.'

On our visit a valve outside on a siphon supplying one of the lakes had also succumbed to the freezing temperatures, prompting lengthy and extensive excavations. In fact the waterworks, cascades and fountains have been the major project of the

last four years. 'It's all in reasonable condition for the first time in seventy or eighty years,' says Simon Howard. 'But there's never any end to repairs and renovation. Two-thirds of the south-east wing needs re-roofing.' He grimaces.

There are two Holbeins at Castle Howard, one of the Duke of Norfolk and one of Henry VIII, a Rubens of Salome with John the Baptist's head, a Gainsborough of Byron's great-aunt who was the 5th Earl's mother (he became the poet's guardian), and several Joshua Reynolds portraits including one of the 5th Earl in the robes of a Knight of the Thistle accompanied by his dog Rover, who made the Grand Tour with him. There is Meissen porcelain, Hepplewhite chairs, and even a white marble altar from Delphi behind which the Oracle herself once lurked.

'It is,' says Simon Howard, 'a national monument.' On the other hand it is also, paradoxically, a family home. Mr Howard roams the place, personally supervising everything with his mobile phone, or sits at the computer in his book-lined study. His wife is a willing partner and, among many other things, does all the flowers herself – sixteen different arrangements twice a week.

On the one hand the operation is thoroughly up to date. The computer system means, for instance, that when recession and the Gulf War struck the British tourist business simultaneously, Castle Howard could revise its predicted attendance figures at the press of a button. There is a brand new cafeteria; a discreetly placed children's playground; an exceptionally lavish souvenir guide-book. On the other hand, says Simon Howard, 'What we offer above all is a wealth of eighteenth-century attraction both inside and outside. We are always careful to preserve the integrity of the place and to remain true to the original intentions of the people who first planned it. We want people who come here to take pleasure in the grounds and in the artistic quality of the interior.'

Part of the popular perception of Castle Howard will inevitably live on in the shadow of Waugh, but despite that one must remember that it is a great original. When Walpole succumbed to the mausoleum he produced a verdict which encompassed the rest of the house and grounds as well and which ran:

'Nobody had informed me that at one view I should see a palace, a town, a forti-fied city, temples on high places, woods worthy of being each a metropolis of the Druids, the noblest lawn in the world fenced by half the horizon, and a mausoleum that would tempt one to be buried alive; in short, I have seen gigantic places before, but never a sublime one.'

An exaggeration, of course. But not a distortion.

BICKLEIGH CASTLE

Bickleigh is my only thatched castle, the perfect fusion of cosiness and castellation with its stark, warlike exterior concealing home sweet home, it is like the ultimate bitter-sweet, a liqueur chocolate with a brittle crunchy outside concealing a soft liquid core.

I happened on it almost by chance. Major Gibbs of Sheldon Manor had suffered a slight stroke and so was struck sadly off our list. I was in the Quantocks interviewing an Air Vice Marshal, couldn't find a place to stay on the tripper-saturated north Somerset coast and headed inland, putting up in Dulverton at a posh pub. Next morning I consulted my bible, the *Historic Houses, Castles and Gardens Guide* published by British Leisure Publications. And lo, Bickleigh, a mile or so south of Tiverton. Within striking distance. Worth a try, I thought, and so I drove on south.

It was well sign-posted. Two inviting pubs sat astride the main road and to the right lay the castle. I crossed the River Exe, swung a left, felt the road disintegrate below the Peugeots tyres, found a car park, parked and walked up the track. Opening time was not until two, but the castle was intriguingly peculiar. The centrepiece was the sort of castle only a child can draw, four square and squat. This tiny toy fort, the original gatehouse, is all that remains of the first castle. Behind it there was a thatched, flower-festooned Devon farmhouse of the sort expats dream of as they sip their Bovril in time to the World Service rendering of 'Lillibulero'. The juxtaposition was not one I had ever encountered before.

I think, however, that what really won me over to this funny little castle was the legend of Bampfylde Carew, the boy who was expelled from Blundells. I didn't know you *could* be expelled from Blundells, though I have to admit that in writing that I am guilty of the twin crimes of snobbery and in-joke. I was educated at a school in the next-door county and we were West Country rivals of Blundells, to whom we thought ourselves greatly superior.

Bampfylde Carew was the son of the rector of Bickleigh and a member of the family who then owned the castle. According to one account he was nothing short of 'majestic' in appearance, with a more than athletic build and 'his countenance open and ingenious, bearing all those characteristical marks which physiognomists assert denote an honest and good-natured mind'. If the portrait in the castle is anything to

go by, this is an untruth. He has a face like a ham, and a roguish ham at that.

Carew was born in 1693 and swiftly developed an amazing rapport with animals. He had a 'cheering halloo to the dogs which, we believe, was peculiar to himself'. One day he led a number of other Blundells scholars in pursuit of a deer which turned out to belong to a Major Nutcombe. The boys trampled the cornfields, killed the deer and then ran away to the Brick ale-house where they fell in with gypsies. Intoxicated with the gypsy way of life, young Bampfylde took to the road and, in a variety of disguises, became the eighteenth century's leading con-man. At various times he stomped the country, sometimes as a shipwrecked sailor, sometimes a demented rat-catcher, once a vicar from Aberystwyth. He was, in due course, elected 'King of the Gypsies' and soon afterwards deported to the Americas by the Barnstaple magistrates, only to jump ship, be rescued by Indians (who sawed off his restricting iron collar) and return to England decked out as a pious Quaker.

Eventually, after a second escape from another ship he 'reflected how idly he had spent the prime of his life; that the good education heaven had vouchsafed him he had only made use of to disgrace his name, and bring sorrow to his relations, and to deceive and plunder his fellow-creatures with more facility. These cogitations so continually wrought upon him that they occasioned a severe bodily illness; on recovering from which he voluntarily yielded his regal authority.'

He died in 1759 and was honoured with eight lines of doggerel:

> King Carew's race at length is run,
> His wanderings are all o'er;
> No more his tricks, nor wit, nor fun,
> Will make the table roar.
> Bickleigh church-yard is now his home,
> Peace rests upon him there:
> And when the final day is come,
> May he no danger fear.

One of his stocks-in-trade was entering the houses of noblemen and pretending to be their long-lost kinsman. He would then racket about the house banging into walls and tearing his clothes, thus raising 'considerable contributions'. Another was to find out if there had been a disaster in the neighbourhood and then pass himself off as one of the tragic survivors. Further 'contributions' ensued. Sometimes he would trick a household two or three times a day in different disguises, male and female. *The Life and Adventures of Bampfylde Moore Carew* describes him as 'The noted Devonshire Stroler and Dog-Stealer', but this does him less than justice. He was a genuine oddball, and I hope Blundells now celebrate him despite the sorry affair of Major Nutcombe's deer. I thought he was too good to ignore.

As I had an hour or so to kill, I wandered along the banks of the Exe to one of the inviting pubs where I lunched off a cold trout and some Muscadet. It was an Indian summer day, baking hot for September. Then I ambled back and joined a small group of stately home buffs paying money to an elderly gent in a blazer who turned out to be the present owner of the castle, Mr Noel Boxall. There was a sign near the entrance which advertised an impending ploughing match and an exhibition of 'roots, hay, silage and corn'. This made me feel dispiritingly effete and towny. Why should I be so superior about an exhibition of roots and silage?

Most of the historic houses I visited were inhabited by ancient families clinging on to their heritage for dear life. Few if any would ever admit that they would prefer not to have the millstone of family bricks and mortar hanging round their necks, but I couldn't help feeling that sometimes they would like to have been bequeathed something vulgar in Barbados. Mr Boxall, however, actually went and bought his historic house. And not one but two. Before living here he was at Purse Caundle Manor in Dorset. What's more he used to be a manager with the Midland Bank. He ought to have known better, although he did admit that he didn't tell the bank that he had bought a castle until the deed was done. He knew they wouldn't approve.

The Carews themselves finally moved out in 1922. 'From then on,' says Mr Boxall, 'the castle had a chequered career, I'm afraid.' He bought it from a Lloyds underwriter in 1969 and found it in a sorry state. Every bit of roof apart from the ancient one on the fourteenth-century gatehouse had to be completely rebuilt. It was impossible to do it without government grants, and that meant opening to the public as a quid pro quo. Even so he has hung on and is easily the longest occupant since the Carews themselves. He has lived there alone since his wife, Norma, died early in 1990, though his son lives in one of the cottages in the complex and has a successful business restoring antiques in a converted cowshed.

The first owner was Alward, a Saxon. Then came the de Bickleighs, who must have built the tiny chapel. They were followed by William de Balfago and the Pointington family, and then the Courtenays, Earls of Devon, took over early in the the fifteenth century. They already owned grander castles, so little Bickleigh was given to younger sons until the cadet line almost petered out with an orphan daughter called Elizabeth. Her grandfather invited his cousin William Carew to move in and look after her, but when she grew up Elizabeth, to everyone else's dismay, fell in love with William's younger brother, Thomas. Thomas was 'young and lusty, of an active body and courageous mind', and he won permission to marry Elizabeth after saving the life of his commander-in-chief at the Battle of Flodden.

The demise of Bickleigh as a fully-fledged castle came in the Civil War, when Sir Henry Carew chose the wrong side. Fairfax, the Parliamentarian general, laid siege to Sir Henry and his Royalists and destroyed practically everything except the chapel

and the gatehouse. Afterwards Sir Henry tried to rebuild the castle as a castle but was understandably thwarted by Cromwell, who wasn't having it. He was forced instead to build in cob and thatch. Thus the curious compromise castle we see today.

Mrs Boxall was a Percy on her mother's side, descended from the Dukes of Northumberland of Alnwick Castle, so, as her husband said, 'It was in the blood a bit.' There are still daguerrotypes of her ancestors in the farmhouse and also her charming collection of samplers, dating back to the eighteenth century. On the buffet nearby is one of the oddest pieces in the house, a doll over a hundred and fifty years old. When you lift her skirts and press a handle she nods her head and darns a sock.

More surprising in a way are the Carew portraits on the walls. There are still Carews in Tiverton, and 'Granny Carew', as she was known to the Boxalls, left the portraits and some furniture to her grandson Geoffrey. He had nowhere to put them and asked if they could find room at Bickleigh. Apart from the notorious Bampfylde, pride of place belongs to Sir Alexander, the family martyr, beheaded at the Tower of London in the Civil War. He made a splendid death, leading the crowd in singing the

23rd Psalm from the scaffold, rewarding the axeman with silver and reciting his mother's favourite bedtime prayer before placing his head on the block.

Another piece of family history is shown on the intricate carved overmantel in the Garden Room. This includes the figure of the poor vicar of St Thomas's, Exeter, who was hanged from his own church tower after siding with the Prayer Book rebels of 1549, who objected to the newfangled *English Book of Common Prayer* which today is so revered by traditionalists.

Over in the thatched barn you can take tea – the house is only open in the afternoon – and visit a number of little museums. There are penny farthings and boneshakers and Victorian rocking-horses which Mr Boxall encourages children to ride. In keeping with the agricultural flavour of the announcement of the great ploughing match you can also inspect a display of 'agricultural and domestic objects'. Another Carew echo is the maritime museum centred on the *Mary Rose*, the great ship which sank under the eyes of Henry VIII as it sailed down the Solent in 1545 and which now lies resurrected at Portsmouth. Her commander that day was Vice-Admiral Sir George Carew. A slightly morbid coincidence is that a relation of Mr Boxall was fourth officer on the *Titanic*. He is commemorated too.

I enjoyed finding out about the dreadful Bampfylde Carew, but I was also delighted to renew acquaintance with Charles Fraser-Smith. Some years before I had interviewed him at his cottage in Bratton Fleming on the other side of Exmoor. The article was prompted by a book he wrote on his wartime exploits when he was the prototype for the character 'Q' in Ian Fleming's Bond books. 'Q', you will recall, was the inventor of all those gadgets with which Commander Bond was from time to time able to escape with one bound – death-dealing devices miniaturized and disguised as umbrellas or bars of soap. Here are their real-life progenitors: a tiny flexible saw hidden inside a shoe lace; a compass in a gold tooth; silk handkerchiefs which when moistened became detailed maps of occupied France; hairbrushes and thermos flasks with hidden cavities. 'He came as a visitor,' says Mr Boxall, 'and when he offered us his treasures, of course I jumped at it.' During the season Mr Fraser-Smith, now well into his eighties, comes over twice a month to sell autographed copies of his books. He does extremely well with them, as well he might with a relatively captive market of between twelve and twenty-two thousand Bickleigh visitors a year.

Bickleigh, as I hope you can see, is a place of rare charm and eccentricity. This, I think, is enhanced by the substitution of thatch for battlements, by the lilypads in the moat and the Gingko by the Gate House. And it must be the only castle in England which a bank manager turned into his home.

Ultimately, though, I shall always remember it for Bampfylde the bad boy of Blundells. Though we should not over-romanticize him. For as Mr Boxall remarked, reflectively, 'Everyone loves a rogue, but he really was a bit of a rotter.'

HIGHCLERE CASTLE

The Earl of Carnarvon lives in a bungalow.

This is the truth but not the whole truth. 'A magic house down a long and twisting drive. Suddenly everything opens out and there is this lake with lily pads,' I wrote in my notes. This hardly does the place justice either. It's only a few miles south of Newbury which, while not exactly suburbia, is hardly darkest Ayrshire. You drive down this private road, claustrophobic with rhododendrons until suddenly there is an explosion of space and shimmering water. It's like passing from a municipal cemetery straight into the Italian lakes. Two gardeners are clipping gently; there is an insect drone. Indoors a butler in shirt sleeves brings coffee, a Jack Russell prowls, a clock ticks. It is rather dark and almost silent. The bungalow, as you might have guessed, is not your ordinary common or garden bungalow. It is by William Kent. The architect who did Horse Guards in Whitehall.

But we are not here to discuss bungalows, however idyllic. The ancestral home of Lord Carnarvon is Highclere Castle, a Victorian *Schloss* designed by Sir Charles Barry. Barry also did the Travellers' and Reform Clubs, but he is best known for the Houses of Parliament. He himself thought Highclere was better than anything else he did and I think he's right. He called it 'Anglo-Italian', while the present Lord Carnarvon endorses the notion of it being 'Jacobethan'. When Benjamin Disraeli first saw it he was practically lost for words, simply exclaimed, 'How scenical!' If you can imagine a sort of squared-off version of the Palace of Westminster plonked down in a park full of massive cedar trees you might get close to reality. The castle is colossally grand and possitively soars. It is a perfect expression of Victorian pomp and optimism, and though manifestly unsuitable for such serious castelline duties as withstanding sieges or imprisoning princesses, it is still, though Victorian, every inch a castle.

Lord Carnarvon succeeded to the title when his father, the 6th Earl, died in 1987. Before that he was Lord Porchester, known, at least to Fleet Street gossip columnists, as 'Porchie' and an object of their attentions because of his close relationship with the royal family. There has been a successful stud at Highclere since Queen Victoria's reign, and since 1969 the present Earl has been racing manager to Her Majesty the Queen. This has meant a high profile in the public prints.

'I'd always wanted to open the house,' he says. In any case the tax problems following the death of his father made it inevitable. Every aspect of the estate appears to have fallen into every conceivable tax category and I got a definite impression of negotiations with the Revenue which were impenetrably byzantine and likely to drag on till the crack of doom.

'It's a real home,' he says of the castle, explaining a touch strangely, 'we use it but we don't live there.'

He set about the opening with some zest, enlisting the help of Norman Hudson, 'an expert on opening country houses', and attacking the problems of going public in as professional a manner as possible. 'The philosophy,' he says, talking now of house and garden, estate and stud, 'is to conserve and enhance the beauty of the place and – within reason – to allow other people to benefit as well as ourselves.' When I visited him he was just embarking on his second open season, but he gave every sign of genuinely enjoying it. He says he is tremendously touched when, as often happens, someone comes up to him and says, 'Oh Lord Carnarvon, thank you so much for sharing it with us.'

The family name of the Earls of Carnarvon is Herbert. Once you've boned up a little on the English country house and the families that live in them you will instinctively deduce that this must mean that they are something to do with the Earls of Pembroke who live the other side of Salisbury at Wilton. The supposition is correct. In 1692 Margaret, Countess of Pembroke, was left a house at Highclere by her father Robert Sawyer. He was a lawyer and a friend of Samuel Pepys at Magdalene College, Cambridge, and Margaret was his only child.

When her husband died, Wilton was left to their eldest son and the house at Highclere went to the second, Robert, and passed to his nephew Henry after his death in 1697. It was this Henry who was created Earl of Carnarvon by George III for his part in quelling the Gordon Riots in 1780.

His grandson, the 3rd Earl, commissioned Barry to design him a castle. Like many of his family he was keenly interested in politics – he was a devout opponent of the repeal of the Corn Laws – but his chief love was foreign travel. He was particularly interested in the Moors and Moorish architecture and wrote a play – tragic – about the Moors as well as a number of poems. His portrait, looking saturnine and pensive in a leathery brown jacket, hangs in the Gothick entrance hall. His new castle can be seen looming behind him. The house that preceded it was Georgian and not, in Carnarvon's estimation, sufficiently grand.

The third Henry lived to see the shell of the house complete but not the interiors. Most of these were designed for his son, another Henry, the 4th Earl, by the architect Thomas Allom. Other interior designers included George Gilbert Scott, who designed St Pancras Station and the Albert Memorial. He did the columns and

fan-vaulting in the hall while rebuilding the parish church. Another eminent Victorian, William Butterfield, architect of Keble College, Oxford, was responsible for the original central heating system. This 3rd Earl is commemorated by linked 'C's throughout the house. One C stands for Carnarvon; the other for Chesterfield, whose daughter Evelyn Stanhope was his second wife. Another recurring motif is the wyvern, which the Oxford dictionary defines as a 'winged two-legged dragon with barbed tail'. The wyvern is the heraldic beast of the Carnarvons.

'My ancestor', said the present Earl in front of one portrait as we toured the castle, 'kidnapped by brigands and murdered by Greeks.' And then again, 'My great-grandfather was Colonial Secretary and Viceroy of Ireland.' This is heady stuff but it is the present Earl's grandfather who has contributed the most eccentric legacy to Highclere. There is a clue to this in the tea-room where there is a Jak cartoon from the London *Evening Standard* in which a butler is shown with three nubile topless Egyptian ladies while a crusty aristocrat enquires of him, 'All right, Taylor, what have you found in the attic this time?'

Not a wildly amusing joke, but there is a point to it, for this unusual piece of Victorian Gothick in unspoiled Berkshire ('the estates between Newbury and Winchester are practically unchanged since the nineteenth century') is the home of a unique collection of ancient Egyptian relics. The place is full of them. Indeed, shortly before my visit another Egyptian find had actually made the front page of the *Daily Telegraph*.

'King Tut relic found at castle', ran the headline.

Not a very high quality newspaper headline, but the story itself was an immaculate piece of *Telegraph* reporting:

'An alabaster head of King Amenophis III, Tutankhamun's grandfather, has been discovered at the ancestral home of the Earl of Carnarvon, whose grandfather led the excavation of the Tutankhamun tomb in the 1920s.

'Mr Leslie Taylor, a security officer at Highclere Castle, Hants, found the three-inch head, similar to one in the Metropolitan Museum in New York while preparing for a tea-room to open to the public.

'"There were some gun racks with green baize bases," Lord Carnarvon said last night. "My security officer found what appeared to be a carving rolling around under the baize."

'Last year, other relics from Egypt's Valley of the Kings unearthed by the 5th Earl and the archaeologist Mr Howard Carter were discovered at the castle. The alabaster head is now on display at the castle with the rest of the collection.'

As the *Telegraph* story suggests, the alabaster head of Amenophis was a bonus. The big find was in July 1987, when Lord Carnarvon decided to unblock the door between the drawing room and the smoking room. In the thickness of the wall he discovered a series of small pigeon-holes containing packages. Hidden treasure. These were relics from the tombs of the Egyptian monarchy and aristocracy. Some of them were more than three thousand years old and the only person who knew anything about them was the previous earl's butler, Robert Taylor.

It's a rum story, worthy of a Rider Haggard at least. The 5th Earl, born 1866, was George Edward Stanhope Molyneux Herbert. The portrait of him at Highclere, painted by William Carter, shows a raffish figure, head and hat tilted rakishly to one side, one hand grasping a lapel, the other a gasper. As a young man he was a successful racehorse owner, a keen photographer and a reckless car-driver with a penchant for travelling at more than 20mph. This proved his undoing, because in 1901 he had a bad accident which left him unsuited for English winters. Because of this he fetched up in Egypt two years later and took up what was then known as 'Egyptology'.

By 1906 Carnarvon had persuaded the head of the Egyptian Antiquities Service, Gaston Maspero, to allow him to dig. Maspero, however, only let him loose in a barren, much dug area, and in his first year all Carnarvon found was a large mummified cat which he presented to the Cairo museum. For the following year Carnarvon took on a professional archaeologist, Howard Carter, and the two of them enjoyed five productive years at Thebes. There was then a barren period followed in 1915 by more success in the Valley of the Kings and the beginnings of a quest for the tomb of the boy king, Tutankhamun. In November 1922 he and Carter found it, intact and stuffed with all the funerary paraphernalia associated with this rich period of Egyptian history more than thirteen hundred years before Christ.

The Herberts of Highclere seem to be a superstitious family. There is an old tradition that if the portrait of Margaret Sawyer, 8th Countess of Pembroke, is moved from its place by the dining-room fireplace a disaster will befall them. So far the portrait has remained unmoved. The tomb of Tutankhamun carried a similar curse and it took effect with devastating speed. Only months after the discovery Lord Carnarvon grazed a mosquito bite while shaving; blood poisoning ensued, followed by pneumonia and, on 5 April 1923, death. The fatal razor and the 'Certificat de Decès' are now on display along with all the other relics. Immediately after the 5th Earl's death the family had tried to destroy all memory of the Egyptian links. Papers and books were destroyed, and Almina Lady Carnarvon sold the bulk of his collection to the Metropolitan Museum in New York. What everybody overlooked were described in a postscript to Howard Carter's inventory in the following words: 'A few unimportant antiquities not belonging to the above series I left at Highclere.' And now they are out from the hiding places and on public display.

The capital costs of getting the castle ready for public display have been well over £300,000, but that implies a commercialism which is slightly misleading. The flowers at the castle, for instance, are done daily by Lady Carnarvon, and though I didn't see her that day I saw her trug lying on a chest alongside a pair of secateurs and knew she couldn't be far away. There have been gardens at Highclere at least since 1218 when the then owner, Bishop of Winchester, planted sixty-one fruit trees. Today the formal walled gardens are imaginatively devoted to such oddities as an entirely white herbaceous border, a bed of scented geraniums between yews, espaliered medlars and quinces, and greenhouses containing grapefruit and figs, grapes and oranges, bananas and rice, coffee and eucalyptus.

It's still a family business. His son and heir Geordie is a partner in the farm, Harry the second son runs Kennet Valley Thoroughbreds, and Caroline his daughter helps as a bloodstock agent. The stud thrives. So does the cricket ground where Keith Miller played. And Ted Dexter and Prince Philip. In its first year 27,000 people came to see it all, though Lord Carnarvon says he is trying to 'keep it upmarket'. They do private dinners and receptions, and Hampshire County Council celebrated

their centenary here. During the war the castle was lived in by evacuees from Brent. Now that it's open to all, some of them have been back to have a look. It also remains, as it has been for years, a fine sporting estate with famous shooting and 'very good angling'. There are sixty or seventy fishing licences and plenty of pike, perch and tench.

In his *Rural Rides* in 1821 William Cobbett described it as 'the prettiest park I have ever seen'. That was before the new castle was built by Barry. Pretty is no longer quite the word. It is magnificent, but not pretty. Too grand by half. And while there is much to admire if I were the Earl of Carnarvon and master of Highclere I think that I too might forgo the castle as a place in which to live. Like him I think I'd prefer the bungalow.

MILTON MANOR

Milton Manor is the Oxfordshire home of the Mockler family and of the Authors' Book Fair, which takes place every year – more or less. Anthony Mockler is a foreign correspondent (best known for his book on mercenaries) turned literary biographer. At the third Book Fair in June 1989 he was a compelling figure with his shock of silver hair, his lightweight khaki suit and his vivid yellow tie. From time to time he would blow shrill blasts on his Acme Thunderer Whistle swinging from his neck or beat out a rhythm on exotic native drums in order to get the assembled authors to queue up for their free Pimms or listen to the beautiful blonde in white who played the violin in the back garden. He was like a bookish scoutmaster of eccentric disposition or the British Council rep somewhere truly forgotten like Bangui or Ulan Bator. Despite his exoticism, there was no questioning his Englishness.

There were about thirty of us authors, each one with a table. It was much like any garden fête, only with a more precise focus. Philip Howard, Literary Editor of *The Times*, tall, myopic, grumbling and erudite, had set out his stall in the shade at the back of the house so that his books were the first to be seen. I set up alongside: my crime and cricket against his history and lexicography. To the left of him Mr D. G. Chandler, dressed as Napoleon, had an inventive display of naval and military books and a miniature cannon, which he discharged at tea, almost deafening Paul Cox who was sketching nearby. Around the corner were novelists Lee Langley and Wendy Perriam, John Bowen and David Cook, biographer Nicola Beauman, and gardener Roddy Llewellyn, in rhubarb and custard braces, not best pleased because his publishers had failed to deliver any books for him to sell. The actress Jane Lapotaire was in a similar position.

After lunch Monica Dickens, celebrating her fiftieth year as an author, declared the fair open and the public began to trickle in. I sold just over £60 worth of book and came equal fourth with Wendy Perriam in a 'mini-Booker Prize' competition to decide which author's book contained the best first sentence. (Wendy's was much ruder than mine – something about a sperm sample in a jar from Fortnum's.) The sun shone; the public fingered the books; the authors pretended to be unconcerned; nobody took it unduly seriously, let alone believed Mockler's prediction that it would ever rival the publishing industry's annual jamboree in Frankfurt. This was writing as a cottage industry – a do-it-yourself business. My sales manager was my son Alexander, who developed a positively Petticoat Lane patter in cut-price bargaining. My mother-in-law was given a book by Philip Howard, he knowing that she did the *Times* crossword. And all the while the house, more like an Osbert Lancaster drawing than any other house I know, beamed on with a proprietorial benevolence. One or two authors and one or two of the public even took the guided tour.

Milton was originally Middletune. Marjorie Mockler, Anthony's mother, told me that a man called Alfwin was the original lord of the manor. He was given the land by Edwy, King of Wessex from 955 to 959, and the Mocklers remain loyal to the idea of Wessex. Anthony has fought numerous elections under the banner of Wessex Nationalism, though without success. The house might still be described by a romantic as being in Wessex, though a more prosaic cartographer would say twenty minutes south of Oxford on the A34.

Alfwin should have begot Bertwin who begot Fredwin, but instead he passed the manor to the nearby Benedictine Abbey of Abingdon. The Abbots of Abingdon held Milton for four hundred years. A lay-bailiff lived in a small house on the estate and collected rents for the Abbots, until they became some of the richest Abbots in England. At the Dissolution of the Monasteries it reverted to King Henry VIII. He held it personally for nine years and then made it over to his Lord Chancellor, Sir Thomas Wriothesley, later Earl of Southampton, a man whom Henry VIII liked to refer to as 'my pig'. (A typical Henry VIII jest – though appropriate – Wriothesley was a notably nasty piece of work.)

Wriothesley only kept Milton a few months. He already owned the former Abbey at Beaulieu and decided to turn a quick profit by selling Milton to a London goldsmith called Thomas Calton. At first the Caltons lived in the old bailiff's house which had been renamed 'The Dower House' (grander). It later became a lot less grand when it was turned into 'The Dog Inn'. Today the Milton village pub still stands on the site but is now called the 'Admiral Benbow'. (The Admiral's daughter married a Calton and he once lived in the house.)

In 1653 Paul Calton, great grandson of the purchaser, 'decided to build a Mansion' a hundred yards to the west of the Dower House. He had married an heiress and was in funds. The Dower House wasn't grand enough for a gentleman with a rich wife. Ten years later the new mansion was complete. This original building is now the centre of the house. This is described by Mrs Mockler's daughter Suzanne, in the official Milton guide-book, as 'a simple red-brick square, three storeys high, capped by a sloping roof with all four elevations absolutely equal and all four sides decorated by pilasters and fleurs-de-lis'. This economic description seems to me entirely accurate. She adds that the front and back are absolutely identical, which is unusual, and

that each floor is constructed on similar lines – a central corridor running east to west with three rooms off, all the same size. The rest of the space is taken up by the original ninety foot high oak staircase.

It is often said that Inigo Jones was the architect, although, inconveniently for this belief, he died in 1652. Mrs Mockler, however, pointed out, with spirit, that his designs were often used after his death and that even if it wasn't, well . . . ACTUALLY designed by him, 'in any case it shows his influence'. Indeed it does. And the Accounts Book of 1764 quite specifically says, 'The Manor House built on a design of Inigo Jones'.

Anyway it was quite dramatically added to in 1764, immediately after changing hands for the last time. The Caltons had got through the heiress's money by then, and the house had to be mortgaged in 1723. The last male Calton was a gay bachelor who went off to live in Hampstead, leaving Milton in the hands of his three unmarried sisters. They gave up the unequal task on 5 October 1764 and sold out to Bryant Barrett, lacemaker and embroiderer of 479 The Strand. Barrett was 'lace-man' to George III, and he got the house for £10,600.

Like Paul Calton, the lacemaker was plainly a wealthy man, though he had made his own fortune rather than hunted it. Despite making lace for the Hanoverian monarch he was a secret Jacobite who had sent money to Bonnie Prince Charlie in France. He was also a Roman Catholic convert and began his occupancy of the Manor with a ferocious row with the rector of St Blaise, the little church just outside the front gate. This was resolved by the end of the decade and the Barretts were even allowed to build a family vault on to the church. Yet more ecumenical, one of the earliest occupants was Bishop Challoner, who stayed there until the 1940s when he was moved to Westminster Cathedral.

After Barrett's first wife had died young, he married Winifred Eyston, a local girl from an old Catholic family, and they had eight children. Just over two months after buying Milton he wrote in his Accounts Book, 'Began the repairs and building'. The work went on for seven years; the builders came specially from London – with the exception of only two locals; and they used 700,000 bricks. At the end of it all the house had acquired two Georgian wings, a new kitchen, laundry and brewery. There was a stable block, a walled garden and three ponds formed by damming the Ginge Brook, a tributary of the Thames. The exterior blends in well with the original – Inigo Jones or not – which was also given new sash windows and doorways. Inside, however, Barrett got his architect, Stephen Wright, and a London carver, Richard Lawrence, to combine on an exuberant Strawberry Hill Gothick library and a chapel which was originally known as a 'Mass Centre'. It has thirteenth- and fourteenth-century stained-glass windows which Barrett bought from Steventon Church for £7. Only direct descendants of the Barretts may be married there.

Two of Mrs Mockler's children were indeed married there. She first came to the house in 1946, when it was given to her by her unmarried uncle, Louis Barrett. His father, Bryant's grandson, known as 'The Guv'nor', was the architect of a financial disaster which led to poor Uncle Louis having to sell practically the entire contents of the house. The Guv'nor was a tremendous railway buff and invented a new kind of steam engine which he patented. Not content with this, he laid down his own railway track in the Manor grounds. Alas, his revolutionary engine never caught on, and complete financial ruin was only just averted.

Despite the sale of the contents there is still plenty of fascinating stuff around. The Steck pianola in the drawing-room was made for Queen Victoria's youngest daughter, Beatrice; the carving of the Last Supper was made for the Great Exhibition of 1851. The family portrait of Anthony's father the late Surgeon Captain Mockler RN (in uniform) in the bosom of his family was painted in the dining-room by Nesta Warren. Everyone looks remarkably stiff and uncomfortable except for the labrador sprawled asleep at Mrs Mockler's feet. A Kneller of the Churchill sisters is on the staircase. The library contains Mrs Mockler's grandmother's dolls' tea set and a telescope which once belonged to Admiral Benbow. There is a Burmese hand-sewn gold and silver peacock in the Chinese Bedroom and an extraordinary eighteenth-century Dutch marquetry bed in the dressing-room. It is supposed to be all one man's work, and it's only sad that neither of Milton's two royal visitors can ever had slept in it. They both came a century too early. William of Orange stayed the night in December 1688, and Peter the Great of Russia came for a whole fortnight after getting an honorary degree at Oxford. He spent the time discussing naval affairs with the famous Admiral Benbow. (Am I unfair in sensing that the Admiral must have been a tiny bit of a bore?) Most of the authors, with the obvious exception of Roddy Llewellyn and Jane Lapotaire, seemed to have an extremely jolly day at the Milton Manor Book Fair. It helped that the sun shone; it helped me that, thanks largely to Alexander, I sold more books that P. Howard next door; it helped that the house has a funny smiling face and that the lunch was appetizing and that the Howards had brought acceptable wine and that the Mocklers were so enthusiastic. Authors, contrary to outside suspicion, get on very well together whenever they meet, and under these conditions everyone got on so well that they resolved to come again next year and bring their friends. We would organize a charabanc and advertise the excursion at PEN and the Society of Authors. Of course, it would never be like the Frankfurt Book Fair, whatever Anthony said. That was so quintessentially German and this couldn't help being so utterly English. We were all looking forward to another hot day in Oxfordshire in June. Sadly Mrs Mockler has since passed away, but in 1991 the Fair was still going strong, with her son Anthony now in charge of house and garden.

SANDRINGHAM HOUSE

It was Sant Dersingham in Domesday though Sant has nothing, as I had originally thought, to do with sanctity. It simply means 'sand'. Dersingham means 'dwelling of the water meadow'. Sandringham, therefore, means that it is a sandy spot by the dwelling of the water meadow. Nowadays Dersingham has been subsumed by its sandy neighbour and has become simply a low-lying village on one of the most famous estates in the world. Sandringham itself is the Royal Family's private home in East Anglia, a favourite retreat for a succession of monarchs. George V, in avuncular mood, once wrote: 'Dear Old Sandringham, the place I love better than anywhere else in the world.' George VI told Queen Mary, 'I have always been so happy here and I love the place.' Edward VII, its original owner, made it his main base for forty-nine years and put his stamp on it so firmly that one former Royal employee said to me, 'It's as if he had never left, just as Balmoral still feels as if Queen Victoria was still alive.' The only King who disliked it was Edward VIII. He wanted to sell it. But other events got in his way. The house stayed in the family and the King, to all intents and purposes, did not.

It was raining on the day the illustrator and I had chosen for our visit, which made it almost unique that summer. The illustrator has recently moved to an enormous old rectory in the north Norfolk village of Tilney All Saints so we drove over in half an hour. As Noël Coward wrote in *Private Lives*, "Very flat, Norfolk". It is, it is,

though the Sandringham grounds undulate perfectly satisfactorily and a plethora of huge Wellingtonias, copper beeches and weeping willows shield the house from the savage winds which beat in across the North Sea from Scandinavia and whip over the fens in winter. In fact the gardens are so soft and sylvan that they don't feel like my idea of Norfolk at all.

We had chosen to call on a Saturday in July during the annual Norwich Union Driving Trials. In some respects this was a mistake. I was killing two birds with a single stone because I was researching a biography of Prince Philip, Duke of Edinburgh and carriage driving is one of his consuming passions. You could almost say he created the sport single-handed, and the Duke was entered in this competition, driving at number 76 in the section headed 'Teams of Four Ponies, under 148 cm'. The entry was engagingly laconic. First the owner: 'H.M. The Queen. Buckingham Palace, London'. then the horses' names: 'Lowthwaite Lady III, Balmoral Bramble, Bannerdale Dawn, Sanja Ebony, Balmoral Cilla.' And finally the equipe: 'Black gelding and mares driven to a Bennington Phaeton by HRH the Duke of Edinburgh.' The Duke is a perfectionist who likes to do things well, and last year he had won the championship. This year, however, he did not.

The house and grounds were not officially open to the public that day, so we had a special pass from Julian Loyd, Her Majesty's Land Agent, to park our car by York Cottage, for over thirty years the home of King George V and Queen Mary, now more prosaically the Estate Office. Then the pass said that we could roam more or less as we pleased, though we were uncomfortably aware of the high security. One was always turning a corner round a rhododendron and finding a closed circuit TV camera.

On this occasion the only people around were the competitors and officials with clipboards and armbands checking to see, for instance, that the horses did not, in certain sections, break out of a walk. Out in the park the atmosphere was like a country point-to-point and the carriages careered round a tight and demanding course complete with such excitements as deep water hazards. But nearer the house they were more sedate. The gentle clip-clop of the horses' hooves, the rattle and squeak of wheels and harness, made an appealing descant to the plangent drip of rain. And the sign of horsedrawn traffic progressing past the enormous Victorian mansion reminded one irresistibly of another era and, inevitably, of Edward VII, the nineteenth-century Prince of Wales. In the house there is an oil painting of *A Big Shoot in 1867* by Thomas Jones Parker. It shows Lord Teesdale VC, the Marquis of Hartington, the Duke of Beaufort, Captain Ellis, Christopher Sykes MP and the Earl of Chesterfield, all posed nonchalantly with guns and whiskers and rakish hats and tweed plus fours and spaniels. In the centre is the Prince of Wales, cigar in one hand, shotgun crooked over his elbow, sporting the most raffish hat of all and a suit of a check so loud not even an American golfer would wear it today. Half close your eyes and you could almost see them swaggering towards you through the drizzle.

Sandringham is a very private house, not, like Windsor Castle or Buckingham Palace, 'vested in the state'. It was originally purchased with money from the tax-free income from the Duchy of Lancaster and the Duchy of Cornwall. And the sovereign is exempt from the death duties which so eroded the possessions of so many of his or her subjects' possessions. No swingeing eighty per cent demands have ever meant crisis at Sandringham. It is also used to receive official visitors and the Queen, who after all never ceases being Queen, does official business here. Yet the conceit is that, like Balmoral in Scotland, it is a 'private' house, while Windsor and Buckingham Palace are not. The finances of the royal family, however, are an arcane and byzantine matter, and we should not get embroiled in them here.

Nevertheless, it is unexpected to find that since 1977, and at the express wish of the Queen herself, it is 'shared' with the public in much the same way as Chatsworth or Hatfield, Milton or Sandford Orcas Manor. By the *porte-cochère* at the entrance there are signs saying, 'Queue here for entry to house' and 'Prams and push-chairs not permitted'. And even though Her Majesty and her family are not in the habit of conducting guided tours around the house, they do feature to a surprising extent in the official glossy brochure. There is even a photograph of the Queen on the cover. Three corgis are rootling around at her feet, there is a sea of mauve rhododendron behind her and she is looking, a touch critically, at some particularly fine primrose yellow blooms which I take also to be rhododendrons. Inside the introduction is surmounted by the royal coat of arms and there are more royal photos: Her Majesty in the drawing-room in front of a picture by Edward Hughes of Queen Alexandra when Princess of Wales – five dogs this time, mainly corgi with perhaps a dash of dachshund in the one who is actually sitting on the sofa alongside its mistress; a smiling Queen (three dogs again) by a magnolia with ponds and conifers in the background; a six-dog picture behind daffodils; a page with three pictures of Her Majesty in the gardens during spring, corgis again present throughout; another with Her Majesty standing in front of the upper lake with the west front in the background, royal standard fluttering against an azure sky; on page nineteen a family group, including the Queen Mother and the Queen's grandchildren, outside Sandringham Church; another of the Queen in the greenhouse with geraniums and the head gardener, with whom she appears to be sharing a joke; and finally Her Majesty at Sandringham Stud holding a filly and foal. A cornucopia of royal photographs for the royalty watcher, though the truth is that when the Royal Family are staying there, the rest of us are not allowed in.

I cannot think of another historic house owner whose image bulks quite so large in its presentation. I cannot think either of an owner whose image is quite so instantly recognizable. All the same, it comes as a bit of a shock. One associates owners such as Lord Montagu or the Marquess of Bath or the Duke of Bedford, before he fled the country for Monte Carlo and New Mexico, with an element of showmanship. It is ridiculous in modern times to be surprised to find the map of Her Majesty's country house full of signs saying 'Souvenir Shop', 'kickabout area', 'coaches', 'lavatories', 'car parks', 'ticket office' and 'main entrance to grounds'. One of the main arguments against opening the Queen's Gallery in Buckingham Palace to the public was that it would be a thin end of the wedge, and before long the common herd would want to see inside the palace itself. Surely Sandringham is a thick piece of wedge?

Never mind, the monarchy remains as intractable a mystery as ever, and a visit to Sandringham does little to diminish it. Although people have lived there since Anglo-Saxon times it has been royal for only just over a hundred years. In 1861 Queen Victoria and Prince Albert decided that their eldest son should have a country house of his own by the time he was twenty-one in two years' time. The poor Prince Consort died before the search was completed but the Queen persevered, and on 4 February 1862 the Prince of Wales and the Keeper of the Privy Purse, Sir Charles Phipps, went to Sandringham to investigate a house for sale. The vendor was a stepson of the Prime Minister, Lord Palmerston, called The Hon. Charles Spencer Cowper, who was moving to France. Phipps reported favourably to the Queen. Exterior ugly, interior fine, grounds pretty, surrounding countryside plain. The whole in good order, recommend purchase asap. The Queen did as she was recommended.

The ugly but convenient house had been built in the late eighteenth century by Cornish Henley, who died before it was finished. His son sold it to a neighbour who left it to Cowper when he died in 1843. Cowper himself tacked on several bits and pieces, mostly built in brick and thin slabs of local carrstone. Only his conservatory was retained when the Prince of Wales rebuilt everything himself and it was turned into a billiard room.

Today, at least on a rainy day, the house has a rather forbidding institutional feel like a very grand private nursing home or boys' preparatory school. Tall chimneys, stone facing setting off brickwork and carrstone. The house feels enormous even though it has been abandoned for Christmas holidays because the extended family does not fit; but Sandringham does have a Victorian shapelessness which, allied to its pretension, I find off-putting. The grounds are still lovely; the walk across them to the tiny parish church would almost make Christmas there a treat. But not quite.

Inside, well yes. The Princess of Wales thought the new ballroom they added in 1883, eleven years after the rest of the house, was 'beautiful I think and a great success and avoids pulling the hall to pieces each time there is a ball or anything'. Queen Victoria thought the main drawing-room, where the family gather for pre-dinner drinks, 'a very long and handsome drawing-room with painted ceiling and panels with two fireplaces'. This is accurate as far as it goes, but it is not a room to warm the heart. It is so very large, with chairs so very upright and uncomfortable looking, and the sense of a very grand hotel in Eastbourne so overwhelming.

As always, I found the little oddities the most appealing. The dogs' cemetery near the sundial, full of Queen Alexandra's favourites, so overgrown I had to scrape away the covering fuschia to read 'Little Billee' and 'Sir Nicolas'. The trees planted by members of the family and recorded in their diaries so simply. '25th April 1889. Out with Bertie, Alix Louise, and all the children, and I planted a tree in front of the house.' That was Victoria and it was an oak. Or 11 January 1936: 'I planted a cedar in front of the house. Evan-Thomas brought the seed home in 1882 when he was with us. It was only found after he died four years ago.' That was George V, only nine days before he too died. Evan-Thomas was an Admiral with whom he served.

My favourite oddity is a tiny summer-house called 'The Nest', very dark, at least on that gloomy day, and tiled within, it contains, on the wall, Tennyson's romantic 'Crossing the Bar' with its famous lament,

> Sunset and evening star
> And one clear call for me!
> And may there be no moaning of the bar
> When I put out to sea.

It was built by General Sir Dighton Probyn VC, a long-serving courtier who became Comptroller of Queen Alexandra's Household after the death of her husband the King. The General's inscription is still there and it reads:

The Queen's Nest – a small offering to the Blessed Lady from Her Beloved Majesty's very devoted servant General Probyn 1913 – Today tomorrow and every day God bless her and guard her I fervently pray.

I am moved by the soldierly simplicity of those sentiments, so much more impressive than any number of priceless tapestries and portraits and Russian goblets or looming staterooms. I can see that it is a failing in me, but the more ostentatious a place the more I try to seek out those things which persuade me that, despite all the evidence to the contrary, the rich and aristocratic and even the royal are, *au fond*, the same as you and me. That is why I like the graves of dogs with pretentious names; and the planting of trees, and unaffected expressions of love.

There is just enough of that at Sandringham to persuade me that I could be right.

SOMERLEYTON HALL

I t was an irresistible invitation. 'Bill and Belinda Somerleyton request the pleasure of your company at a Crossley Gathering at Somerleyton Hall on Saturday 15th July 1989. 12 Noon. Lunch and Tea. RSVP Lord Somerleyton, Somerleyton Hall, Lowestoft, Suffolk.' I responded in the affirmative, drove early to Liverpool Street Station and was thwarted. Unlike sensible stations like Waterloo and Paddington, Liverpool Street has nowhere to park. Goodness, what a laugh the policeman had when I asked if he knew where I might leave the car. One should not go on about the unspeakable bloodiness of London Transport, London traffic, London parking and the sheer horror of getting from A to Z in our capital city when attempting a celebration of the English country house. All the same it was astonishing how many of my visits were marred by their beginnings and ends.

In the event I did not get to Somerleyton until over a year after the Crossley gathering. The house was closed to the public but there was a BBC TV crew on the rampage in the maze; Lord Somerleyton (Bill) was off in Scotland getting in a spot of fishing; Lady Somerleyton was unwell and had taken to her bed. Never mind, the

younger generation were in residence. The Hon. Alicia made us welcome and showed us round. She was about to start her third year at Newcastle University. She was a jolly, breezy girl and her relaxed irreverence was refreshing.

'How was the Crossley gathering?' I asked her.

'Oh fine,' she said, 'Dad got rather over-excited.'

You see what I mean. Her attitude to Mum, Dad, home, and life itself reminded me of my own daughters. That afternoon she was being made to go into Great

Yarmouth to see the Royal Shakespeare Company do *The Taming of the Shrew*. It was the last thing in the world she wanted to do, but Mum was insisting. Mum, by the way, is the sister of Willy Loyd, the great polo buff and retired Major. I had met the Somerleytons once briefly at Willy's house. When I mentioned this to Alicia I became instantly promoted from a mere jobbing writer to 'a friend of Uncle Willys'. I felt rather a fraud, but I am sure Major Loyd would have been amused.

Alicia's surname is Crossley and the Crossley gathering was a reunion for a hundred and fifty or so of her kin from all round the world. The original Crossley fortune was founded on carpets from Halifax, and Somerleyton Hall is an expression of nouveaux riches. It is not, however, the house that Crossley built. The Crossleys only came in 1863, by which time the house was already complete.

The site had been occupied since the early thirteenth century when Sir Peter Fitzosbert built a house in about 1240. In 1320 Isabel Fitzosbert, the family heiress, married Sir Walter Jernegan, and the Jernegans stayed for thirteen generations until 1604 when John Wentworth took over and rebuilt Somerleyton as a conventional East Anglian Jacobean mansion. It remained like this until the mid nineteenth century, passing through the hands of the Wentworths, the Allins and the Anguishes until the last of the Anguishes died in 1843.

This was when the modern history of Somerleyton Hall began. That same year the estate was bought by Sir Morton Peto. Sir Morton was an archetypal Victorian. As an apprentice bricklayer he had learned the building trade the hard way, laying eight hundred bricks a day. Then at twenty-one he inherited half of an uncle's modest building business and transformed it into one of the leading contractors of the day. Peto built railways in Britain, Denmark, the Argentine and Russia. Peto built the Houses of Parliament and Nelson's Column, and on a more local and domestic level laid out the new harbour and esplanade in nearby Lowestoft. At one stage he was reputed to be the biggest single employer of labour in the entire world.

He was only thirty-four years old when he bought Somerleyton. In 1847 he became Liberal MP for Norwich and in 1855 he was created a baronet. He had transformed himself: bricklayer to baronet in a quarter of a century.

The house which was to reflect his transmogrification was the work of John Thomas, a young protégé of Sir Charles Barry and Prince Albert who was responsible for much of the carving in the Houses of Parliament as well as the huge lions – eighty tons each – which crouch at the entrance to the Britannia Bridge over the Menai Straits. Thomas built the dairy at Windsor Castle and did a palace on the Bosporus for a Turkish Sultan. For Morton Peto he completely revamped the old Jacobean house. It seems that Peto wanted a Jacobean style while Thomas favoured something more Italian. To my untutored eye it looks irredeemably and unmistakeably what it is – a proud boast of a self-made Victorian gent. There are deer with antlers standing on the gateposts; beside the entrance to the stables is a cupola-topped clocktower; while at the other end of the Hall there is a tall campanile with a room which used to be a smoking room and observatory. It used to be said that you could see the sea in one direction and Norwich cathedral in the other. When Alicia took us up there, clambering over some almost prehistoric Arnold Lunn-type skis to get up the narrow spiral staircase, we could see the sea but not the church. Alicia was keen to have a dinner party there, but Mum was not enthusiastic. Bit of a fire risk.

The clock over the stables has a lovely tinny chime and is the work of Vulliamy, the clockmaster to Queen Victoria and several of her immediate predecessors. It was originally intended for Parliament and might even now have been inside Big Ben. In 1847 the House of Lords moved that a clock be designed for Parliament and Vulliamy was asked to design it. When he submitted the first model it was found to be too expensive and elaborate, so the Lords put the job out to competition. Vulliamy was piqued by this and refused to compete. Sir Morton, perhaps feeling some responsibility for the débâcle, bought Vulliamy's clock and built the splendid stable block tower to house it. Morton Peto's greatest extravagance, however, was his Winter Garden. It was demolished in 1914, but in its day it was one of the most fabulous conservatories in the country – 126 feet by 136. The present Somerleytons dream of restoring it but it would be stunningly expensive. For a recent party, however, they did recreate the effect by tenting in the pretty sunken garden with its lily pool and fountain which is the sight of the original *folie de grandeur.* There was dancing round the pool and no one fell in.

Alas, before he could really enjoy his Suffolk creation, Sir Morton Peto fell on hard times. His debts in 1861 were £4 million and in 1866 he went badly bankrupt. In 1863 he was therefore compelled to sell his cherished house and estate to another eminent Victorian, Sir Francis Crossley, better known to his friends in Halifax as Frank. Sir Morton, incidentally, lived to be eighty, though to what extent his fortunes revived I simply do not know.

Frank Crossley's father, John, started the carpet business, working his way up from weaver to foreman to fully-fledged mill-owner. Then Francis, Joseph and John succeeded him and in 1851 took out a patent on a new steam-driven loom which revolutionized the carpet industry., Suddenly carpets became common. Everyone could have a carpet. The world-wide boom turned the Crossleys into millionaires, but they remained as they had always been – 'hard-working, open-handed, chapel-going Yorkshiremen without much education but with plenty of sense and no pretensions.' They were much given to philanthropy, and Frank apparently liked to include in his speeches a little homily about his wonderful mother. He was MP for Halifax and later the West Riding of Yorkshire from 1852 until his death in 1872.

In the days of his youth Frank was a fiery radical who fought against the House

of Lords, the Established Church, primogeniture and privilege in all its forms. Yet he bought one of the most ostentatious stately homes in the country, accepted a baronetcy and sent his son to Eton.

What went wrong?

There is an extent, I suppose, to which the acquisition of riches can turn almost any egalitarian radical into a thorough-going reactionary, but even so the sudden change in the Crossleys is quite startling. It seems to have had something to do with his wife, Martha. Martha's family were also in carpets, but they were Brintons from Kidderminster. Martha did not like Yorkshire and she had serious social aspirations. These were swiftly realized. Not only was she the lady of the manor, and a spectacular manor at that, her son Savile was Paymaster-General, a Privy Councillor, a Lord-in-Waiting to King George V and crowned a career of successful public service by being created the first Baron Somerleyton in 1916. His son and grandson (the present Baron) have never sought to emulate this public profile but have tended to stay home and concentrate on running the estate and being pillars of the local community. They have become indistinguishable from squires who came over with the Conqueror.

We were let in round the side by Alicia, but had we come in through the front door we would have been confronted by polar bears, a brace, shot by the present Baron's grandfather in 1896, two of fifty-seven massacred in a mere five weeks. The bears are all very well but the centre-piece of this room is a Carrara marble figure of the first Lord Somerleyton as a child. He looks far too good to be true. In one hand he holds a hatful of shells, in the other a spade. He is clearly sitting on the beach at Lowestoft.

Beyond this entrance hall there is a 'staircase hall' replete with family portraits, all of which could have been done by Osbert Lancaster. Also an H. B. W. Davies of *Highland Cattle*. The Scottish cows look rather bedraggled. As always I steer clear of bovine portraits and zone in on esoterica. In this case I was amused by the royal or semi-royal pictures: not just our own dear Queen, and the Kings of Spain and Norway, but Nancy and Ronald Reagan too. The interior is surprisingly domestic. Was it a good idea to shave the ceiling off the twenty-eight foot high banqueting hall to make new bedrooms? The whole top floor of Somerleyton is now unused. The library which has been born from the wreckage of the banqueting hall is snug enough but a little gloomy, and the lowered ceiling does, well, lower.

For a house with such panache on the outside the interior is surprisingly austere. Too much panelling, not enough window. There are treasures to be sure – a fine Joseph Wright of Derby in the Dining Room and a landseer specially commissioned for the Hall by poor Sir Morton. It is called *Stag, Hind and Calf* and all right if you like that sort of thing. Stag looks rabid to me.

It was a lovely Indian summer day and I confess I was relieved to get out of doors. Alicia was not as knowledgeable as her parents might have been but she had exuberance and it is endearing to have someone point at a house like Somerleyton and say, without a hint of pretension, 'That's my room there, under the tower, the one with the bay window.' A sense of belonging does wonders for houses such as this.

The gardens are spectacular, despite the TV crews with their cables. 'I'm lost,' said one waif, knocking at the door as the illustrator sketched the polar bears. 'Where are the BBC?' Alicia remembered other TV crews: *Tales of the Unexpected* with Gielgud and Joan Collins; *Nanny*, because one of the nanny's boyfriends lived here. The storms just touched here and in a corner of the Paxton greenhouse there is an exhibit of dead trees – a two hundred year old copper beach, a hundred and fifty year old lime. And there have been other depredations. 'We've had all our lead babies stolen from My Lady's Garden,' said Alicia. She was right. Someone had nicked the cherubs from their plinths. Unfortunately the family were not that keen on the lead babies and did not mind enough about their departure. Or so it seemed to me.

In the stables the heir to the barony, the Honourable Hugh, was doing something professional with a saddle. He is off to Cirencester soon to learn about the theory of farming. It was nice to see stables actually working; equally it was nice to see a house of Victorian elegance and exuberance. The illustrator sketched in the old glassed passage overlooking the Winter Gardens. I wandered on the lawns, relaxing for a moment on a semi-circular bench let into the wall. 'Look,' he said, when I returned. And he gestured at two nymphs, cavorting topless by the plastic tables and chairs. I looked. They were well sculptured, statuesque, agreeably naked from the waist up.

'Castanets,' said the illustrator.

He was right. Both girls had castanets, and I realized as I noticed it that this was the great attraction of Somerleyton. In all sorts of ways and at all sorts of times it lets itself down and remembers its shop-floor Halifax origins and becomes splendidly and inimitably vulgar. Polar bears in the hall, Nancy and Ronald's souvenir photograph, castanets on the nymphs . . . The thought made me even more resentful about missing the Crossley gathering. I like the idea of an over-excited Dad with a hundred and fifty carpet-baggers, but even so I enjoyed Somerleyton: brass to barony in one bound. Pity though about poor Sir Morton Peto.

RAGLEY HALL

'One of the lovely things about having a Chippendale desk,' said the Marquess of Hertford, 'is that everything works'.

There is no point in owning Chippendale desks, Capability Brown parks, beds slept in by royalty, innumerable portraits by Sir Joshua Reynolds and a seventeenth-century Florentine bronze horse unless you enjoy them. And one of the lovely things about Hugh Edward Conway Seymour, 8th Marquess of Hertford, Baron Conway of Ragley, Baron Conway of Killultagh, Earl of Hertford, Viscount Beauchamp, and Earl of Yarmouth, is that he so obviously enjoys all that he surveys. His Chippendale desk is a case in point, and he slides the drawers in and out, demonstrating the smoothness of movement with the delight a small boy would take in a new electric train.

The desk sits in his study at Ragley Hall, a magnificent Warwickshire pile first built for his ancestors in 1680. The rest of the furniture in the study was actually made specially for this room over two hundred years ago, though the two settees and four chairs were sold in 1921 to help pay off some punitive death duties. In 1971 they were returned by their then owner Lord Bearsted, who felt the stuff 'ought to be where it belongs'. An act, says Lord Hertford, 'of quite exceptional generosity.'

The illustrator and I were a shade late for lunch. Trains from Paddington to Evesham were in disarray and the illustrator, driving from Norfolk, ran into traffic jams near Birmingham. It was a grey damp misty November day and the russet woodlands splashing through the monochrome reminded the Marquess of Monet and the illustrator of Turner. Warwickshire always looks good according to Lord Hertford, but apart from the fact that this weather curtailed the vistas, he thought that this sort of day was best of all. It was log-fire weather, though we did nip out on to the long balcony on the west front outside the Green Drawing Room and gazed across the rose garden towards the woods through which, twenty years ago, Lord Hertford cut a dramatic avenue to improve the earlier parkscaping of Capability Brown.

The gates were shut when we arrived, and the great house had a mildly deserted air. Stomping across the gravel we ascended the swirling steps, passed under the massive columns and portico added on in 1780 by James Wyatt, through an open french window and into an astonishing hall.

It was being prepared for a lunch party the following day – something to do with

an incentive scheme for company employees – with round tables and gilt chairs, more than a hundred of them. Clay pigeon shooting in the morning, clay pigeon shooting in the afternoon, and luncheon in one of England's authentically grand rooms; seventy foot long, forty wide and forty high. It was designed by James Gibbs in 1750 and has busts of the Prince Regent by Nollekens and of the 2nd Lord Hertford by Count Gleichen. It is one of the grandest rooms in all England, and too good in all conscience for a clay pigeon shooters' lunch. We had just entered it, tentatively, when across it, languidly, strolled our host, the 8th Marquess, in open-neck shirt and tweed jacket, ruddy faced from a morning's riding. He looked as if he should have been smoking a cigarette through a holder, and he would have been up until a year or so ago, but he gave up smoking and put on two stones, whereupon he also gave up waterskiing on the grounds that fat men should not be seen in public without protective clothing. He is not, of course, fat, just not as wafer-thin as previously. But the hanging up of his water-skis is sad for the paying punters because he used to give demonstrations on his lake. Indeed, in *The Gilt and the Gingerbread,* the book I helped Lord Montagu write in the Sixties, we included a picture of the water-skiing Marquess by his friend Patrick Lichfield. Very elegant he looked too.

We arrived at the Hall to find a mild crisis. One dog, a phlegmatic Great Dane called Homer, was in place, sprawled floppily on the floor, but his companion, a young Belgian shepherd called Jacques, had gone AWOL. This was highly uncharacteristic and the Marchioness was agitated. The Marquess, however, thought we had better have a drink. He went to a wall of leather-bound books and, swinging a section of it open, revealed an impressive drink cupboard.

In 1966 Lord Montagu said, a shade unkindly, that Ragley's 'comparative lack of success in attracting a large number of visitors is impossible to explain'. At the time Lord Hertford was a Swinging Sixties' figure with his own public relations agency. He is rather evasive about his old image, but his wife, the former Louise de Caraman Chimay and a countess in her own right, insists that is its true. He even, by way of proof, features in a glossy Lichfield photo of the day which includes all the trendiest men about town.

In any case, success in the historic house business is relative. When the Hertfords first moved into the house in 1956, their friends and family thought they were mad and gave them three months at the most before they came to their senses. Lord Hertford had succeeded to the title and the house when he was only nine years old, but during the war Ragley had been commandeered as a hospital. Then he and his mother moved out to a farmhouse, and his trustees in their wisdom advised that the Hall should be demolished as soon as possible. They were finally overruled, but even when the Hertfords had got Ragley into good enough shape to open to the public it was not exactly in pristine nick. A team of government inspectors turned up to see if they might qualify for a grant. 'They found that every single room open to the public was "derelict",' says the Marquess, 'and that two others were "totally derelict".'

They have deliberately preserved one small jumble room in the state in which they found it, just to demonstrate the magnitude of the task which confronted them. It is a depressing sight. Not only is the decay omnipresent and apparently terminal, but the decor, such as it is, has all been carried out in a colour traditionally known in my family as 'monkey dung'. The paper is hanging off the walls and the only lights are antique gas jets. At first they camped in three rooms upstairs. I am surprised they lasted three months, let alone more than thirty years. 'We had nowhere else to go,' says the Marquess. 'People used to say to us, "Why don't you live in a house you can afford to live in?" How boring! What would you do all day?

We lunched off partridge peppered with just enough lead to demonstrate that it was the real thing and shot on the wing. As the pictures in the private dining-room demonstrate, this is a sporting family, now and always. The Marquess rides to hounds twice a week with the Pytchley and always on Saturdays.

The first mention of Ragley is in 711, when the King of Mercia gave the manor to Evesham Abbey. Its origins are not, however, as splendid as that implies, nor as its present architectural beauty suggests. Ragley is apparently Anglo-Saxon for rubbish dump. Seven hundred years later a small castle was built on the site, and in the reign of Queen Elizabeth I this was bought by Sir John Conway of Conway Castle. This was the last time Ragley was bought and sold.

Charles II made Sir John's great-grandson an earl, and it was he who commissioned the building of the present house. However, the family did not move in until the middle of the following century, preferring to stay in 'the Old Hall' which stood where the present rose garden is. Lord Hertford thinks this may have been because they were too busy with other estates in Wales and Ireland, or because there was simply a shortage of funds.

The estate passed from the Conways to the Seymours through a chapter of accidents typical of English family history. The 1st Earl of Conway died leaving no sons; his only daughter was engaged to a cousin called Popham Seymour who was killed in a duel; so after her death Ragley went to his younger brother, Francis, who was made Baron Conway by Queen Anne. I am painfully aware that this sounds like something from Sellar and Yeatman's *1066 and All That*, but that is, very briefly and simply, how it happened.

Baron Conway's son Francis was the 1st Marquess of Hertford, and his portrait by Sir Joshua Reynolds shows a public figure of great distinction in a red coat with fur collar, a mane of grey hair, an imperious look with a trace of humour about the lips and what I assume to be the star of the order of the Garter on his chest. He was Lord Lieutenant of Ireland, Ambassador to France and Lord Chamberlain of England.

His son, the 2nd Marquess, was friendly with the Prince of Wales, though not as friendly as the Marchioness, whose name was linked with the Prince's despite the usual protestations of 'just good friendship'. After the Prince's accession to the throne she was asked if he had ever discussed her apparent successor, Lady Conyngham. Lady Hertford produced a reply which would have been grist to the mill of a 1990s gossip columnist. 'Intimately as I have known the King,' she said, 'he has never ventured to talk to me about his mistresses.'

The 3rd Marquess was also an intimate of the Prince of Wales. Married to the heiress Maria Fagniani, who was left a fortune by both the Duke of Queensberry and Lord Selwyn because each man believed her to be his illegitimate daughter, he used the money to lay the basis of what is now known as the Wallace Collection and to conduct a later life of extravagant excess. He is supposed to be the model for Lord Monmouth in Disraeli's *Coningsby* and for Lord Steyne in Thackeray's *Vanity Fair.* His son, the 4th Marquess, spent all his life in Paris and all his money on pictures. The great art collection was left to his illegitimate son, Richard Wallace, who in turn left it to the nation. It remains open to the public and, as *Michelin* would say, 'worth a detour'.

The 4th Marquess was succeeded by his second cousin who restored respectability to the line while eschewing the extravagant artistic licence of his immediate forebears. He sold the other family home, Conway Castle, and their property in Coventry, and, for the first time in years, Ragley and the estate received some serious attention. He became equerry to Prince Albert and Lord Chamberlain to Queen Victoria.

The Marquesses of Hertford are an unusual mixture of aestheticism and squirearchy. Hugh, the 6th Marquess, was a hunting and shooting man. His son, George, was interested in the theatre and the arts. Hugh was so distressed by this that he disinherited him in favour of the more stolid second son, Brigadier Lord Henry Seymour, father of the 8th Marquess, who was – is – the present holder of the title, my host at lunch, that autumn afternoon when the dog went missing and was unable to eat our left-over partridge.

'Let's have coffee in the Green Drawing Room,' said Lord Hertford. And he led the way through the house like the butler who was not with us. The moveable feast reminded me of an All Souls' dinner, a progress from one historic room to another, pausing from time to time to savour food, drink and different surroundings. The Green Drawing Room is his favourite, and we were joined here by the wandering Belgian shepherd, all bushy-tailed and smiling-jawed. Also rather uncontrollable.

The view from this room is 'one of life's privileges', the portraits are practically all by Reynolds except for a van Loo of Field-Marshal Henry Seymour Conway; the china is mostly Meissen; the grandfather clock was made by Joseph Knibb in 1680;

the carpet was a present from Princess Alphonse de Chimay, the present Marchioness's mother, and was specially woven in Portugal in 1973. One of the attractions of this room and of this house is that it is a fusion of ancient and modern, most of it created as a one-off present for Ragley and therefore unique and uniquely appropriate.

'In our first year,' he says, 'we did get one or two complaints that we weren't worth half a crown.' He smiles. 'That was a little hurtful.' The exterior of the house, of course, was no better than the inside. The stone was flaking badly – 'And as it comes from underneath Birmingham it's rather difficult to replace.' Another of the Maquess' self-deprecatory grins.

When Lord Montagu wrote so rudely about the low attendance figures they were pulling in about forty thousand visitors a year. 'We did rise to the giddy heights of 117,000 in 1979 to 1980, which was about 17,000 too much. Then a severe decline set in and we're currently at about 75,000 or so. There is a slight difference of opinion between the Marquess and Marchioness about how many visitors the house can stand, but as the Marchioness says, 'No house was constructed for all those feet all going in the same direction.'

Apart from the ordinary paying public there are other ways of making money, such as the clay pigeon shoot and lunch. That weekend they were entertaining sixteen travel agents. It has not always been successful. 'Do you remember those beastly Germans who took my ash tray? On one occasion I was taking round a small private party and getting not a glimmer of a response, not even to my tiny jokes. After about half an hour of this agony the courier finally told me that none of them spoke any English. And there were those people who powered into the drink cupboard and said "where's the popcorn?" And the couple from Florida who kept saying how tiny the park was. They used to spread the marmalade on the bacon. They could not understand that it was a house, not a hotel.'

After years of sticky dinner parties the Marchioness discovered that she need only ask two questions to provoke prolonged and animated discussion: 'Where have you come from today?' and 'Where are you going tomorrow?'

As a result of all this, however, the house is in better condition that it can have been for years. Not only that, they have added their own defining touches, nowhere more obviously than in the vast Graham Rust mural which covers the whole of the south staircase hall and shows, in addition to the devil tempting Christ on the Mount of Temptation: all four Hertford children with their parents and godparents, and various Ragley touches such as peacocks, the owl that lives in the oak tree, and the distinctive 'Ragley penstemon' which the Marchioness describes as a 'beautiful raspberry foxglove'. Not being a gardener I knew nothing of penstemons, but my Oxford dictionary says: 'A genus of herbaceous plants of the Natural Order *Scrophulariacaae*,

natives of America, having showy clustered flowers, usually tubular and two lipped, and of various colours.' This extraordinary painting was begun in 1969 and is still not quite complete.

Restoring Ragley has obviously been a struggle. 'It is difficult to avoid whinge-ing,' concedes the Marquess, 'and, of course, we're much richer than most people. But if you own a house as big as this with a hundred rooms, some of which are very big then you're bound to run out of money from time to time. But the two of us have had a much more interesting and enjoyable time than if we had moved into an easily manageable house.'

It is obviously now a marvellous place in which to live on a day-to-day basis, though the Marchioness says it was ten years before she could bring herself to call it home. But it is at party time that it really comes into its own. There was a huge bash in the summer of 1990 when the Marquess celebrated his sixtieth birthday and his eldest daughter, Lady Carolyn, her thirtieth. And there was to be another in December that year, shortly after our visit, when the Ragley son and heir, the Earl of

Yarmouth, was getting married in Alcester parish church. It was to be an evening black tie affair followed by dinner at the Hall.

Then the following year the Earl and his new Brazilian bride were due to move in and take over the baton from his parents.

'That's the point,' says the Marquess. 'You hand on the torch to the young and they too put their stamp on the place. The house is like a book. You turn a page and the whole thing goes rollicking on!'

It is an appealing image, the idea of the English country house as fine leather-bound volume, with every generation setting its print on its own particular chapter. Some fifty years ago the Hertford trustees wanted to slam this book shut, but thanks to the labours of the last few years it looks good for many pages more.

GUNBY HALL

We lunched at the Massingberd Arms on the fringe of the Lincolnshire Wolds. There was me and the illustrator and Hugh Montgomery-Massingberd. Hugh and I met at Kings Cross, stopped at Grantham for a lightning tour which included the birthplace of Margaret Thatcher (née Roberts), now a Routier restaurant, and were picked up by the illustrator at Boston, home of the Stump. Hugh is incorrigible. We had a half-bottle of champagne on the train for breakfast and then at the Massingberd Arms he spotted a dish called 'The Massingberd Grill'. We had one each: a beef steak, a gammon ditto, a pork chop, a kidney, a banger, some liver, mushrooms, tomatoes, chips. The Massingberds are true trenchermen.

'John', said mine hostess to mine host, 'This is squire's cousin.'

Hugh beamed.

And here we should pause to take stock. You may not be aware of Hugh Montgomery-Massingberd, but he is even more of a national treasure than the ancestral home towards which, via the ancestral pub, we were slowly heading. He is the Obituaries Editor of the *Daily Telegraph,* and has in a paradoxical way breathed enormous life into those previously bleak and reverential columns. He is also a writer in the tradition of G. K. Chesterton, Hilaire Belloc and Sir John Squire, devoted to all the good things about traditional England. Massingberd's charm is enhanced by his bulk. On the day of our excursion to Lincolnshire he had managed by ruthless dieting to cut his weight from almost nineteen to just over sixteen stone. He had also broken a couple of toes by bumping into furniture in his London flat. This, you must understand, is a man who fell into the urinal at Chesterfield station while on his way to interview the Duchess of Devonshire. Whatever else he may be, Hugh Montgomery-Massingberd is not run of the mill.

Had things panned out he would be squire-in-residence at Gunby Hall. Gunby is the Massingberd house. Well, it is ONE of the Massingberd houses – the other is the one opposite the pub where we had lunch and is occupied by his cousin, Massingberd-Mundy, a bachelor and former submariner who resigned his stewardship at Market Rasen after a row with the Jockey Club.

Gunby Hall, the house in question, presides in neat seventeenth-century authority over an estate just outside Skegness. Like Massingberd-Mundy's house, it once had a Massingberd Arms hard by the park gate, but Hugh's ferociously teetotal aunt closed it down many years ago and it has never reopened. Hugh's ancestors have been here or hereabouts since at least the fifteenth century, while the earliest reference to a Lincolnshire Massingberd is in 1288, when Lambert Massingberd was convicted on a grievous bodily harm charge. Unlike Hugh, who is by nature unaggressive, the family have often been bad-tempered and warlike. The name itself, Anglo-Saxon for ginger beard, evokes in my mind a vision of generation upon generation of whiskery warriors, culminating in the last real Massingberd of Gunby, Field-Marshal Sir Archibald, of whom more later.

It was Thomas Massingberd who got hold of the Gunby estate in 1495 by marrying the local heiress. He was knighted at Anne Boleyn's wedding and is buried in the tiny church beyond the garden. His memorial brass is there too, and very fine, though Hugh says it is a hundred years older that the date of his death and might have been his grandfather's. Many Massingberds are buried in the crypt, but latterly it was sealed off and more recent generations have gone to earth. Recently, however, another difficult cousin, Freda, left instructions in her will that she wished to be buried in the crypt like the early Massingberds. The burial was a most unpleasant experience for all concerned and no one wishes to repeat it. The crypt is accordingly now sealed for good.

The sixteenth century saw the Massingberds at their most powerful and prosperous. Sir Oswald belonged to the Order of the Knights of Malta and was its Grand Prior of Ireland. He was imprisoned for pulling off another knight's beard, and was also charged with stealing a slave and her daughter, killing four slaves and conspiring to murder the Grand Master. To this last charge he responded, 'I did well to kill the slaves but in not having at the same time killed the old and imbecile Grand Master, I did not do well.' In his official guide to Gunby Hugh tells us that one historian says Sir Oswald was 'of somewhat querulous disposition'. His nephew was the last ever Member of Parliament for Calais.

In the Civil War the Massingberds fought on the Parliamentarian side to such effect that Sir Henry was made a baronet by Cromwell. I don't recollect any mention of Cromwell creating baronetcies when Christopher Hill was trying to teach me seventeenth-century history, but that's probably my fault. Nevertheless, it seems a most unCromwellian activity. Even more surprisingly, Sir Henry was recreated a baronet by Charles II after the restoration of the monarchy.

Gunby Hall itself was the creation of the 2nd Baronet, Sir William. He originally lived in Batoft Hall but knocked it down and built himself a better house on the other side of the park. He used red brick, some of which came from Holland, some from a quarry in what is now the Icehouse Pond. The brick is decorated with Ketton stone, which came from Rutland by barge but despite the occasional twirl the

finished article is a touch puritanical though, as Hugh says, 'saved from austerity by a pleasingly quaint provincialism'. It changed hardly at all until the end of the nineteenth century when the north wing was added. This was essential because the house's single water closet was no longer enough.

Meanwhile the family fortunes waxed and waned. There is, I need hardly say, a Massingberd curse. A Massingberd lady went off with a groom. The wronged Massingberd male set off in pursuit and slew the groom and he with his dying breath cried out, 'May no Massingberd succeed his father.' And none ever has. The family tree zig-zags down the years like a deranged helter-skelter, skipping from cousins to aunts with a reckless abandon, acquiring hyphens and dropping titles with manic zeal. One Massingberd even settled in Russia and moved to Finland so that today there is even a Massingberd clan in Helsinki. They and their English cousins exchange cards at Christmas.

The greatest treasure of Gunby is the only autographed copy of Boswell's *Life of Johnson*, inscribed to Bennet Langton, a Massingberd in all but name. It is dedicated to 'his very faithful and obliged friend' 'The Authour' (sic). Tennyson was once a friend of the Rev. Algernon Langton Massingberd, who painted the poet smoking a pipe. Tennyson wrote about Gunby:

> . . . an English home-grey twilight pour'd
> On dewy pastures, dewy trees
> Softer than sleep – all things in order stored,
> A haunt of ancient peace.

Ralph Vaughan Williams sang here, and another poet who passed this way was John Betjeman, who came to interview Hugh's great-aunt, then in her ninetieth year. Not a happy occasion. 'I hear you write doggerel, Mr Betjeman,' she said to the bard.

Every self-respecting old family not only has its ghosts but its black sheep. There is a portrait of Gunby's black sheep in the dining-room overlooking the lawns. He is in what looks like the uniform of a young naval cadet and he is posed self-consciously against rocks of Gibralterian immensity. Even in extreme youth he looks pretty bad. There is a twist to the lips, an elfin evil in the eyes. A self-serving entry in the marvellous Gunby book of trees which records every planting in the estate's history tells his story in his own words, though a successor has scribbled in a tart corrective about how he sold practically every valuable in the place to finance an extravagant lifestyle.

His memorial is in St Peter's Church without the garden wall. 'Sacred,' it says, 'to the memory of Algernon Massingberd, who is supposed to have been shot at Fort Tabatinga on the Amazon River July 1855 in the 27th year of his age. Placed by his mother Caroline.' Oh, the Curse of the Massingberds! Was he shot or did he drown?

No body was ever found. Perhaps even now there is a tribe of ginger-bearded Amazo-nion Indians, the Massingberdi, roaming the remains of the rain forest. No one will ever know. But he almost ruined Gunby.

We were late arriving at the Hall. The Massingberd Grills at the Massingberd Arms had detained us. Hugh had told the Wrisdales that we would arrive at two, but we were nearer three. The Wrisdales are the tenants. The Wrisdales have lived at Gunby for more than twenty years and have ploughed money, time, energy and love into making the place as neat and tidy and well repaired as it has ever been. Hugh and they are friends, despite the oddity of the arrangement. Every year Hugh spends a summer holiday at Gunby with his family. For the rest of the time the Wrisdales, Jack and Betty, live in the house and are the lords of all they survey, except for the uncomfortable fact that they are all in hock to the National Trust. For Gunby alone among the houses in this book is a Trust house.

It was the Field-Marshal who brought this about. 'This is my uncle in his Field-Marshal's togs,' said Hugh in the dining-room as we halted smartly before a martial figure with a distinct look of Olivier playing at being a Field-Marshal at the Old Vic. I am no military historian, but I cannot escape the feeling that as Field-Marshals go Field-Marshal Sir Archibald Montgomery-Massingberd was not a crashing success.

In 1936 he retired to Gunby. Field-Marshals, of course, never retire, but it seems that in the build-up to the Second World War Sir Archibald's services were no longer required. The old boy went back to his Lincolnshire estate and pottered, and one day out pottering he came across a chap painting white lines on trees. When asked in soldierly terms what he thought he was doing the chap replied that he was marking out the new runway for RAF Gunby. Gunby was to become an airfield, a bastion of the nation's defences against the Bosch.

The Field-Marshal was outraged. He put in a call to the Chief of the Air Staff, his old friend Sir Archibald Sinclair. An almighty row ensued. How, on the one hand, could an old solider like Sir Archibald not make the sacrifice of giving up his home to defeat the Nazis when young men were giving their very lives in that cause? What, responded the Field-Marshal, were we supposed to be defending if not places like Gunby Hall, the very backbone of Old England?

The Field-Marshal won, but it was a Pyrrhic victory. In 1944, sadly, he sold out. Literally. Gunby Hall became the property of the National Trust. Of course, without the Trust many houses like Gunby would be razed to the ground and vast tracks of beautiful countryside would be covered in caravans. But this was sad, because clearly the Field-Marshal was worn out by his altercation with the War Ministry, by a career which despite its apparent success had turned to ashes in its moment of glory, and, not least, from the sound of it, by a singularly forceful wife. Another teetotaller, she used to preach anti-drink sermons to the tenants from a boat in the middle of the Ice

House pond. Teetotalism was not to the Field-Marshal's taste. He liked a dram.

One can't help feeling that in the matter of the Trust the old soldier funked it. He died in 1947, but his indomitable wife lived on till 1963. She was, in Hugh's words, 'erect, stately, unforgettable, forceful, energetic, commanding, outspoken.'

It was then that Hugh's own parents came to Gunby. It was not an unqualified success. Hugh recalls the whole house being 'covered in this horrible sage green paint', but it was not just the paint which depressed them. Although the Trust owned the house and were, in effect, responsible for it, this did not mean that the tenants lived there free. It turned out to be an impossibly expensive exercise. Besides, the house is inconveniently remote from London if that is where your base is. Worst of all were the relations between the Trust's servants and the Massingberds. Perhaps this was inevitable. Both parties must have felt that they should have been in charge of Gunby and the way it was run, but the impossible state of affairs is best summed up by one succinct recollection of Hugh's. One day his mother went into the garden to pick a sprig of parsley. Next day the head gardener, a Trust employee, presented her with a bill. 'To one sprig parsley, two pence.'

It was hardly surprising that the Massingberds moved out. What is fun is that against most of the odds Hugh Montgomery-Massingberd has been able to retain such close links with a house he so plainly loves. All afternoon we roamed its rooms and traipsed around its gardens, pausing here and there to examine some fragment like a Lear cartoon (another family friend) or inhale the scent of the last of the summer flowers. Hugh recalled how, in church one day, the vicar had a seizure and he, Hugh, had to take over the conduct of mattins; also how, with friends, he had dressed in armour and gone clanking to the main road at the bottom of the park in order to demonstrate to the public that the Massingberd ghost was alive and well. We eyed the grass tennis court, the surface deteriorated since the family's stay earlier in the year. We read the Kipling set in the garden wall. Even Kipling, dammit, was a friend of the family and Field-Marshal Sir Archibald was a pall bearer at his funeral.

> Our England is a garden
> And such gardens are not made
> By singing Oh how beautiful
> And sitting in the shade.

Hugh pondered this for a while and said that on the whole he thought he was a sitting in the shade sort of person himself. And finally, while the illustrator sketched, the two of us adjourned to the kitchen for tea with the Wrisdales. We ate cake and a tart. How could we after the Massingberd Grill? And the Wrisdales told us about the concert which raised five hundred pounds for the Skegness Lifeboat and about the prospects for the pheasant shooting. And finally, sadly, it was time to leave.

The sun was setting as we walked across the stable yard and under the clock-tower Hugh's great-aunt picked up in a country house sale near Southampton. Hugh was heading back to the big smoke and another day at his desk in Dockland dealing with the *Daily Telegraph* Obituaries. We paused under the clock and read the Massingberd family motto: *Est mervisse satis* ... 'It is enough to have deserved.'

Not really, I thought to myself, as we walked across the drive and the dolls' house outline of Gunby Hall shrank behind us. It is not at all enough to have deserved and not been given. Hugh, surely, deserves Gunby, Gunby, surely, deserves him. One day, let us hope, the two will get what they deserve.

Who knows, he might even reopen the Massingberd Arms.

HATFIELD HOUSE

Whenever I think of Hatfield I think of the Queen's stockings and *Twelfth Night.* Not this Queen, of course, but Queen Elizabeth I. Lots of great English houses have beds she slept in, but Hatfield is the only one I know of which actually has the stockings that encased the royal legs. There is a garden hat and a pair of gloves, too, with very pointy fingers. She apparently left them behind at a place called Shadwell Lodge while on a visit to Norwich in 1578. All of them are canary yellow, which is why, of course, I think of *Twelfth Night* and poor Malvolio who is fooled into thinking that 'My lady loves me' because she 'commended my yellow stockings of late, she did praise my leg being cross-gartered.'

I suspect this particular piece of Shakespearean larking about had its origins as a royal in-joke. The Queen's silk stockings are believed to have been the first ever worn in England and as such must have achieved some notoriety. I tried this theory on my daughter who is reading English at Oxford and she thought it remarkably nifty and was going to try it out in an essay at the earliest opportunity. I hope it impresses the dons as much as it impresses me.

The Queen's silk stockings are just one of many indications that Hatfield is an authentically grand palace inhabited by an authentically grand family. For over four hundred years the Cecils have been one of the most powerful and influential families in the country. It is not many that can boast of three different Prime Ministers in their family tree. Lord Burghley was Elizabeth I's Prime Minister. His son Robert, the 1st Earl of Salisbury, was James I's, and the great Robert, the 3rd Marquess, was three times Queen Victoria's. His statue, green with verdegris, stands by the pub outside the main gates to the park. 'Erected,' says the inscription, 'to his memory by his Hertfordshire Friends and neighbours in recognition of a great life devoted to the welfare of his country.'

The illustrator and I passed this monument on our walk up to the house. We had come by train from King's Cross, a mere half-hour journey. As the guide-book says, the station is dead opposite the gates and the walk through the park is short and pleasant. The park is still beautiful and gives the impression of remote if cultivated countryside. But the estate is much diminished. 'The New Town took a lot,' says the 6th and present Marquess. 'There are about three to four thousand acres in all. We farmed it until this year but I'm afraid it's not very good land so we've climbed on the bandwagon and gone over to "set aside", which means that the Government pay you not to grow anything on it.' The Marquess looked a little rueful.

The park, of course, is a pleasure garden and the Cecils have shared it with the local population for as long as they have been here. 'Every year,' he says, 'we get about 85,000 paying customers round the house and about sixty in the park and garden. The Hatfield people come in for nothing – that's anyone living within the old parish boundaries. We issue about ten thousand annual passes.'

On the whole people are pretty well behaved, but occasionally there are waves of vandalism. 'Gangs of youths climb in at night and destroy the maze or throw old pots into the swimming pool.' A favourite game is setting fire to ancient hollow oaks. 'It goes up like a chimney,' says the Marquess, looking even more rueful. 'Someone once took an alabaster figure from the chapel. I can't think how. It weighed half a hundredweight. And one of the security guards once found a chap with a whole bag full of cuttings from the garden. He seemed to think it was perfectly allowable.'

The Hatfield brochure has a history of the house written by one of the family, Lord David Cecil, the biographer of Beerbohm and Melbourne, Professor of English at Oxford and one of those legendary civilized dons who brought Eng. Lit. alive for generations of undergraduates. This means that the Hatfield history is rather more elegantly composed than those of most of its rivals.

It hasn't always been a Cecil house. The first building on the site was the Old Palace built by Cardinal Morton, Henry VII's Archbishop of Canterbury and Chancellor (born at Milborne St Andrew, educated at Cerne Abbey and Balliol, and thus eligible for the Galpin Scholarship for those born and educated in Dorset. Or would have been had he lived a few hundred years later. I feel some affinity with Morton because I was a Galpin scholar myself).

Morton's palace was, in Lord David's words, 'a big quadrangle of russet brick'. One side of it, containing the Old Banqueting Hall, is still standing and in use for Elizabethan banquets. 'Serving wenches in costume and Elizabethan players make a really enjoyable evening's entertainment with excellent food and wine cooked in traditional Elizabethan style.' Hmmm. When I mentioned the banquets to the Marquess he said something it would be unfair to repeat.

After the Dissolution of the Monasteries Henry VIII took the Palace over as a home for his children. Lord David, with masterly understatement, says, 'They led a troubled life there.' Mary was there, and waved vainly to her father as he rode past with averted face after her mother Catherine's divorce. After Anne Boleyn's execution her daughter Elizabeth was kept in the house without the clothes to make her decent – no silk stockings and garden hat then. Later Henry mellowed, and she and her half-brother Edward pursued a rigorous classical education there. However, after her

father's death the fifteen-year-old Elizabeth was accused of having an affair with Lord Admiral Seymour of Sudeley but did not wilt under cross-examination. Seymour was executed, but Elizabeth was exonerated.

In 1558 she was sitting under an oak reading when the news came of her sister's death. The Queen is dead; long live the Queen.

'It is the Lord's doing and it is marvellous in our eyes,' she said, which sounds unsisterly but understandable. She then sent for William Cecil, later Lord Burghley, and appointed him her Chief Minister. The first council of her reign was held at the Hall in Hatfield, but after that the Queen spent less time at Hatfield although, as Lord David writes, 'She had left such a mark on the place as makes her still its presiding genius.' There are two portraits of her there – the 'Ermine' by Hilliard and the 'Rainbow' by (probably) Isaac Oliver. The latter shows her in the ultimate Big Sister dress. It's gold, and covered in black ears and eyes to suggest that the Queen is able to see and hear every one of her subjects, no matter what or where or how or when. A chilling garment.

James I, who succeeded Elizabeth, did not share her affection for Hatfield and instead coveted the house of his first minister, old Burghley's son Robert, Earl of Salisbury. This was a place called Theobalds, near Enfield, later destroyed by the Cromwellian army during the Civil War. James proposed a swap. The King being the King, Robert could not refuse, but he didn't like the Old Palace either, and it was he who knocked down three sides of the old russet brick quadrangle and built the present house for £38,000.

The main designer was Robert Lyminge, though the ubiquitous Inigo Jones is thought to have had a part in modifying his designs, and the first 1st Earl of Salisbury himself, hunchbacked and sickly, was a keen amateur interferer. The centre block was grand and set aside for state entertainment; the two wings were more domestic. And poor Salisbury did not live quite long enough to see the house finished.

Lord David Cecil was realistic about his forbears. The Cecils of the next two-and-a-half centuries 'were not men of eminence'. Nevertheless they held a title and they inhabited a great house, so great men and women came to call. They were not always welcome. When James II, then Duke of York, fled from anti-popish demonstrations in London the 3rd Earl would have nothing to do with him. The house was deserted and James had to send out for food and candles.

The 4th Earl was a Jacobite who went to the Tower for his loyalties; the 5th took no part in politics. Nor did the 6th, but he was satirized by Pope and Hogarth for taking on the position of coachman on the public conveyance between Hatfield and London. Driving a coach seems an odd thing for an Earl to do, but having once interviewed a viscount who worked as an assistant in a supermarket, I am not altogether surprised. Still, the 6th Earl does seem to have been ahead of his time in egalitarian terms. A rake and a spendthrift, he. 'Not a credit to the family,' says Lord David.

The 7th Earl was an altogether more substantial figure who became George III's Lord Chamberlain and was rewarded for his services by being created the 1st Marquess. His wife, Emily, the 1st Marchioness, was the stronger character. A renowned Tory hostess, she held all-night gambling parties, went around doling out alms for the poor from a velvet bag held by her groom, and hunted until almost eighty. Half blind and strapped to her horse, she was egged on by the groom shouting disrespectfully, 'Damn you, my lady, jump!' She redecorated and refurnished the house and perished tragically in extreme old age when fire broke out in the west wing. There is a Romney of the Marquess and a Reynolds of the Marchioness. She looks terrific: it would have been marvellous to have been invited to one of her all-night parties.

The 2nd Marquess also gave parties but destroyed his mother's redecorations and substituted it with some ersatz 'Tudorbethan'. He also made the maze and the Tudor gardens at either side of the house. I notice, incidentally, that when Lord David Cecil writes of the maze and the house he gives them both capital letters: the Maze, the House. I don't think that's the correct style and hope I will not be thought guilty of lese-Cecil for putting them in lower case.

The 3rd Marquess made the Cecils great again. Britain too. 'The last Prime Minister to sit in the House of Lords,' wrote his successor, Winston Churchill, 'he had presided over an unparalleled expansion of the British Empire.' He added that when he died 'A certain aloofness of spirit, now considered old-fashioned, passed from British politics.'

'A certain aloofness of spirit, now considered old-fashioned' is an apt phrase for the Cecils. I sensed it with the present Marquess as he described the house's modern persona, its grappling with the contemporary tourist industry. 'We felt our way,' he said, 'took advice from some so-called "leisure experts". We did have some rather awful old cars. They're going. Now we have model soldiers.' These are the pride of his administrator, a military man. They also stage an annual craft fair, quality to begin with not much better than the cars but now much improved. That brings in thirty thousand people in May. Then in June/July there's a sort of mini-Chelsea Flower Show. 'That's when the garden is nearest to its peak.' The latest is a patchwork quilt show. 16,000 predicted. He looked a little bleak, I thought, at the prospect of the patchwork quilt show and I thought also how very dark his suit, how very black his shoes. He was courteous and friendly and helpful but I couldn't help remembering, with a frisson of amusement, that 'certain aloofness of spirit, now considered old-fashioned'.

The last Cecil Prime Minister, the man for whom the phrase was coined, had the chapel redecorated and began the custom of holding a daily service there. He also put in a telephone and electric light. The lighting circuit was dangerous, the wires exposed. Occasionally they would catch fire in the Long Gallery and the family, conversing below, would chuck cushions up to extinguish the flames and carry on talking. Very Cecil. The family at that time included a remarkable group of individuals. James, the eldest son, later the 4th Marquess, was Leader of the House of Lords; William became Bishop of Exeter; Robert won the Nobel Peace Prize; Edward was financial advisor to the Egyptian Government; Hugh became a baron in his own right and was Provost of Eton. Maud married Lord Selborne and was famous for good works, and Gwendolyn was her father's secretary and later wrote his biography. So the conversation under the exploding exposed wires should have been coruscating.

The 5th Marquess, commonly known as 'Bobbity', was the third successive Marquess to be Leader of the House of Lords and was for years the prime *éminence grise* and kingmaker of the Conservative Party. The present, 6th Marquess, is a quieter figure, though he was briefly a Conservative MP (for Bournemouth West), and President of the Monday Club. He exercises a benign influence over the right-wing eponymous *Salisbury Review* and, of course, over his heritage.

'The house is,' he signs, 'beginning to suffer from too much traffic.' Cracks were appearing in plasterwork. In the garden the grass was turning to dust, especially in the gateways. They were experimenting with a honeycomb plastic mesh below the earth's surface. 'A major rehabilitation programme was begun by my father in the mid Fifties,' he says. 'He did the roof. He used copper which is cheaper than lead.' The authorities objected, of course, but when they consulted the original documents they found that at the first building lead was ruled out for the roof on grounds of economy. They used copper instead. 'So copper's fairly traditional,' says the Marquess. All the windows have been replaced, and when I was there the north front was covered in scaffolding. They were putting in a damp course – the first ever.

Hatfield was closed to the public that day, but when we had finished chatting to the Marquess we were allowed to wander about at will through both house and garden. They both felt slightly eerie and some of the portraits are oddly haunting – the two Elizabeths, Mary Queen of Scots, done by Nicholas Hilliard shortly before her execution. Mildred, Lady Burghley, looks extraordinarily fierce. How strange to find the Hat and Shield of Menelik, Emperor of Ethiopia – a trophy of the Victorian Prime Minister's, no doubt. The armour in the armoury belonged to men of the Spanish Armada. In the Long Gallery there is a picture of Lord Burghley riding his mule. Also signed photos of Queen Victoria reading, of Lord Wavell and of Winston Churchill. Ghosts everywhere, ancient and modern.

Outside we came across the Marchioness, a famous gardener, a horticultural adviser to royalty indeed. She was consulting the head gardener, David Beaumont. Mr Beaumont explained in greater detail the problems with grass and bemoaned the fact that the camomile in the herb garden 'won't take the wear and tear'. Apparently the problem of grass and the public is a hardy perennial at the regular meetings of the Professional Gardeners' Guild to which all the great stately home gardeners belong. We were interrupting Mr Beaumont's pruning. There are at Hatfield 106 different sorts of apple tree. I had no idea there were so many different sorts of apple in the entire world, let alone at Hatfield.

I was also delighted to find a working Real Tennis court. Unlike the Dukes of Wellington and Richmond, the Marquesses of Salisbury have done the right thing by the game. 'We put it in order,' says the Marquess, 'and then we said to the players, OK it's up to you. They've done up the club room and the changing-room and they've got a professional. It's a very thriving club. I used to play myself until I damaged my hand. Two of my sons play when they're here.'

In a difficult world the Marquess is cautiously content with his period of ownership. It has changed greatly since he knew it as a child. He remembers six housemaids, two valets, three footmen, various boys, four kitchen maids, even an 'oddman' whose job consisted almost exclusively of carrying firewood. In the old days they all lived in, whereas nowadays most of the staff are part-time and come in from their homes. And running the house as a commercial enterprise with a paying public is a departure which has necessarily meant a change in character.

'I take the view that it's an uncertain future. But I've got it in order and everything's now run in a much more professional manner. You pretend to be amateur, of course, but you aren't.' He paused. 'On the other hand we don't provide theme parks . . . whatever they are.'

Did I detect, for a moment, 'a certain aloofness of spirit, now considered old-fashioned? I do believe I did.

BRYMPTON D'EVERCY

harles Clive-Ponsonby-Fane has to be one of the more remarkable monikers in the English language. It reminds me of A. A. Milne's 'James James Morrison Morrison Weatherby George Dupreé or of someone P. G. Wodehouse would have stuffed into a leather armchair at the Drone's Club. If I put it in a novel there would be protests about my facetiousness.

It is a name which plainly couldn't exist and yet there, on a sunny Somerset afternoon, was its owner dressed in sensible boots and sweater doing something agricultural with a horsebox and a dog at his ancestral home. He looked like a member of the rural squirearchy with his monkish grey tonsure and general air of mucking-out. I was horribly late for our appointment, but it didn't appear to bother him in the least. I felt that even if this was not a man for whom time stood still he was not exactly a man for whom it was a winged chariot.

The house, just outside Yeovil, has been in the family since the early eighteenth century, and rejoices in a name which is almost as exotic as that of its owner: Brympton d'Evercy. I first visited the place because of a newspaper article I was writing about I Zingari, the greatest of all wandering cricket teams. Charles CPF's ancestor Sir Spencer Ponsonby was one of the founders. Spencer added the second barrel to the family name though the addition perplexed even his fellow cricketers. As one remarked of him, in the pavilion at Lord's: 'He who (why I can't explain) to the honoured name of Ponsonby has added that of Fane.'

Brympton today is a cricketing shrine full of I Zingari treasures and heirlooms. In one of the fireplaces there is a stuffed bird which looks like an Imperial Russian Eagle. Round its neck is a bow-tie in the IZ colours of black, red and gold. 'Out of darkness through fire into light.' The room is called the Trophy Room. I particularly like the album in the glass case which opens with the words. 'Cricket is the national game of England and without doubt the grandest game in the world.' I am aware that not everyone who reads this book will share this view, or even understand it, but in considering the historic English house it is one which should be taken into account.

The house is neither big nor grand nor classically correct nor dramatically situated. It is also a little tumbledown. The owner, sitting in his office, a jumble of riding tackle and skiing gear, saw-blades, old socks and bottles of his 'Brympton Apple

Brandy', fresh on the market, remarked forlornly that English Heritage had just 1.4 million to disburse among privately-owned houses such as his. 'Our roof alone,' he said, 'will cost two million to put right.' Despite their air of mild dilapidation and humdrummery it has a magic. At the opening of his brochure CCPF quotes an article by Christopher Hussey in *Country Life*.

'Which is the most beautiful place you have seen?' Hussey asked in rhetorical vein. Almost every house, he claimed – and he is an expert – had something, whether architectural, sentimental, historical or scenic, that made it 'incompatible'. The purist in me thinks he ought to have stopped there, because in truth these houses are so genuinely incomparable that comparisons are, if not odious, at least impossible. But he does go on, and he says: 'Brympton has them all and unites them so perfectly that the whole cannot be surpassed: scarcely be analysed. There are greater, more historic, more architecturally impressive buildings in grander scenery; but I know of none of which the whole impression is more lovely. None that summarizes so exquisitely English country life.'

Well, it's a point of view, and I caught a glimpse of its truth when I, tritely, mentioned to CCPF what a marvellous place it must be for his young children. He seemed faintly surprised. 'It's just home as far as they're concerned,' he said.

Exactly.

The original owners, in the thirteenth century, were the d'Evercy family. They built part of the modest Ham-stone parish church which stands outside the garden wall, and also the Priest House. This has changed very little since then. Indeed, until recently the floor was still earth and you could have grown mushrooms in it had you been so inclined.

About two hundred years later John Stourton bought Brympton as a dowry for his daughter when she married John Sydenham, founder of the second of the three Brympton dynasties. The Sydenhams were the prime architects of the house which survives today. The west front, my favourite, is Tudor and has Henry VIII's coat of arms, a conceit to which they were entitled because of a rather obscure royal marriage involving the Stourtons. You can still see the Sydenham crest, which involves rams, and there is a clock in good working order, reputed to be the oldest such timepiece in the West Country. Below it is another coat of arms which, rather typically, has been put on upside down.

The south front is seventeenth century and quite different. This is Inigo Jones Grand and was commissioned by another Brympton owner with a splendid name, Sir John Posthumous Sydenham Bt. Actually it isn't really Inigo Jones, it is more like 'school of Inigo Jones'. Indeed, he cannot even have supervised the work, because it wasn't begun until 1678 and he died twenty-six years earlier. This was not the first time I had come across such a confusion. The official Brympton brochure is

refreshingly candid about it. 'Architecturally,' it says, 'it is a disaster.' The centre-piece of the façade is a drainpipe and there is a pointed lintel over the window at one end and a rounded one at the other. Tiddly widdly widdly, no symmetry, no symmetry! My own view is that such eccentricities enhance rather than diminish the house's charm.

The Posthumous Sydenham family lived up to his name and died in 1692. Five years later his son Philip was trying to sell what he described as a 'very large New Built Mansion, which had cost £16,000'. Poor Sydenhams. In their heyday they had been the largest landowners in England. By the end of their ownership they had been compelled to mortgage the estate for £50,000. There were no buyers, so Brympton passed into the hands of the Receiver General of Somerset. This was Thomas Penny, cousin of another impossible name, Onesiphorus Penny, the famous Yeovil hatter.

Penny made a number of improvements to the house but, 'being remiss in his returns to the Exchequer, the house was exposed to sale'. The purchaser was Francis Fane MP, a barrister. The law paid well, then as now, and he was able to find £15,492. 10s, which was enough to defeat all rivals at auction.

Francis Fane eventually left his house to his younger brother, who became the 8th Earl of Westmorland. The house was Westmorland property until 1857, when a spinster daughter, Lady Georgina, took over and ran the estate with her trusty agent – another good Brympton name – Mr Blacktop. Poor Georgina was unlucky in love. Her father forbad the marriage she craved, because her soldier suitor was beneath her. He was a subaltern called Wellesley, later the 1st Duke of Wellington. Lady Georgina consoled herself by putting in the pond, laying out the formal gardens, planting thousands of oaks and negotiating the sale of land for what later became the Yeovil to Taunton railway line. She dealt directly with Isambard Kingdom Brunel, and it seems Brunel got the better of her because when she died in 1875 the house was once more in debt.

Her nephew Spencer Ponsonby, the founder of I Zingari, was also her godson, so he inherited the estate despite having an elder brother. He was initially a reluctant heir, but when he saw Brympton for the first time he swore that he would pay off every last penny and sell everything he had rather than part with the house. He was as good as his word and lived there until his death in 1915. Sir Spencer was a man of parts: Palmerston's private secretary, comptroller of the Lord Chamberlain's office, a voracious collector of shoe-buckles (on which he became the country's leading authority), cricketer and father of eleven children. It was he who personally brought home the Treaty ending the Crimean War. When he arrived in Whitehall he found the Foreign Office closed so he left the Treaty with a cleaning lady who was washing the front step, and went off for breakfast. And, of course, it was he who changed Ponsonby to Ponsonby-Fane. A true Victorian.

Spencer's eldest son, John, died a year after his father, leaving a son, Richard, and a daughter, Violet. Richard spent most of his life, on doctor's orders, in Japan and never married. Violet played hockey for the West of England, rowed for Leander, was a master carpenter and a brilliant landscape gardener. It was her son Nicholas who inherited the house from his uncle and added the third barrel, Clive, to the family name. In 1956 Nicholas decided that living in the house was too expensive so they moved to the Rectory behind the stable block, letting the house to Clare School.

The present owner, Charles CPF, moved back in July 1974 after the school went bust. His father had died in 1963 and he had been happy enough to continue with letting to the school. When they left, however, he decided to move back in.

It seemed a good idea at the time, but when he actually moved back in he wasn't so sure. 'The house was empty, totally empty. No bustle, no chatter, just a vast silence that crept into the big rooms. Rooms that I remembered proudly replete with their many possessions, smugly aware of their handsome good looks, had been stripped by the sale and then by the school, to make way for classrooms and labs. And now even those had gone, leaving nothing but chalk dust, ink spots and a feeling of shabby, tatty despair.'

CCPF doesn't actually talk quite like this but he does write like it. The passage is taken from a slim racy volume he published himself under the title *We started a Stately Home*. He continues: 'The gardens, once internationally known, were a shambles: over-grown with negligence and neglect. The Brympton of my youth was no more and never would be again.'

The Brympton of his maturity is still a beautiful place, though the owner expresses his survival in robust terms. 'It's bums through the door that count,' he says. If he could get thirty thousand bums a year he could survive. He has hit twenty-two thousand, has slipped to eleven and in 1990 was running at around fifteen. The recent accolade of 'garden of the year' awarded by Christie's has brought helpful publicity, but he wages a constant battle against the National Trust's Montacute House just a mile-and-a-half down the road. On the one day a week that Montacute is closed, Brympton's attendance increases dramatically. The Trust may not mean to be acquisitive, but its modern marketing techniques, its national membership scheme and its huge resources mean that Brympton is always likely to lose out in this local Somerset derby.

To counter this he is employing all the entrepreneurial skills he can muster. 'It's because of these skills that people like us are still in houses like these,' he says. Thus the vineyard producing palatable Château Brympton, and thus the apple brandy, a bottle of which I purchased for £14.50, and which I drink as I write. It is good, a more than acceptable answer to French Calvados, a mouth-tingling response to the historical skills and probity of customs and excise, an intoxicating riposte to the plenitude of Plymouth gin, traditional tipple of West Country drinking folk. Three thousand bottles of Brympton applejack a year will surely triumph or he should know the reason why. His house is also in increasing demand as a photographic location. Lord Lichfield – Patrick – is a frequent visitor. Brympton features in Japanese mail order catalogues.

'It's the three 'W's that make the difference,' he says, quoting another owner. 'The will, the wealth, the wife.' He has the will and the wife, the indefatigible and supportive Judy, though the wealth is more problematic.

For nearly seven hundred years there has been a religious building on the site of tiny St Andrew's Church which blends in to the Brymptonscape, giving it a touch of divine timelessness. Cromwell knocked about the faces of the saints in the stained-glass windows and old Sir Spencer moved the font to accommodate the ample frame of a fat washerwoman, but it remains a tiny Ham-stone intimation of immortality. An inscription on one of the tombstones reads:

> Remember me as you pass by
> As you are now, so once was I
> As I am now, so must you be,
> Therefore prepare to follow me!

CHATSWORTH

The Duchess of Devonshire maintains that if you live in the same place for a long time you become 'hefted to your hill like an old sheep'. It's a splendidly felicitous phrase, as you'd expect from a Mitford, and you know immediately what she means, except that anyone less like an old sheep is difficult to imagine. She is much more like one of the grander species of jungle cat, even on a Derbyshire hilltop in a houndstooth skirt and a scarlet cardy. She has the same piercing light blue eyes as her sister Diana Mosley, though despite being a Duchess she is less alarming, less angular, the laugh lines less austere. A good writer, too. That phrase about the sheep comes from the arresting first sentence of her book about the Chatsworth estate, a sequel to the one she wrote ten years earlier, in 1980, about the house. The two are invaluable to anyone who really wants to know about one of the grandest ducal properties in all England.

I originally approached Chatsworth through the Marquess of Hartington, aka 'Stoker', or 'Sto' for short. I knew him briefly and vaguely at university where we both, improbably, belonged to the same club – the Gridiron – a run-down undergraduate imitation of the Garrick and White's where Christ Church aristos and Balliol subversives eyed each other balefully across the dining tables. Stoker, like another unlikely member, the champagne revolutionary Tariq Ali, came from Exeter College but was and looked and the most blue-blooded member of all. His curious nickname derived from his childhood ambition which was to be an engine-driver. He is now Senior Steward of the Jockey Club.

Stoker passed me on with a recommendation to his father, which is how and why one early autumn noontide the illustrator and the illustrator's wife and I came to be drinking the Duke's sherry in the Duke's sitting-room. It is actually more of a study than a sitting-room, but when pressed on this point the Duke said disarmingly that he spent more time in it sitting than studying. It's easy to see why. The view from the window across Capability Brown parkland to the steeple of Edensor Parish Church is incomparable. The Duke has written his memoirs, though he thinks they are too dull to publish. The title is 'Privileged View'. He has a dust-jacket design to prove it and I can see why, sitting at his window, he finds it difficult to do anything other than stare out at England and contemplate.

He was wearing a pink neckerchief, for he is a raffish Duke with an elderly elegance and leftish, almost Bohemian tendencies. There is a bust of Charles James Fox in his room; the shelves are stacked with modern books of his own collection, from Wodehouse to contemporary political biography; he even resigned from the Conservative Party, despite having held office under his relation, by marriage, Harold Macmillan, to join the SDP. Macmillan was staying in the house the night the night-flowering cactus flowered in the Paxton greenhouse some time around midnight. His deputy agent, Roger Wardle, remembers the telephone call summoning him to witness this rare moment and how the Duke stood under the glass gallantly presenting the exquisite blooms to his lady guests. He is that sort of Duke.

His house, however, is not that sort of house. Some English houses are so much part of their history and their environment that they have an almost organic quality as if they had grown generation by generation like the oaks in the park; some have religious origins; some were built for war. Chatsworth, more than any other home I know, strikes one as a shouted challenge of wealth, power and status. It is far from ugly, though I don't care for the Kremlinesque section at the north which was built on by the 6th, bachelor Duke at the beginning of the nineteenth century. But with Chatsworth the aesthetics of the building are somehow secondary. It is the power, the arrogance, the assertion of this huge building which takes the breath away, especially in the context of a bucolic Derwent valley, studded with sheep and cattle, so peaceful, quiet and essentially unassertive.

The roof of the house covers just over an acre and the roof of the stables only a little less. There are one hundred and seventy-five rooms, fifty-one of them enormous. They include twenty-one kitchens. The three hundred and fifty-nine doors are connected by seventeen staircases and three thousand four hundred and twenty-six feet of passage. The three hundred and ninety-seven external window frames, the sixty-two internal ones, the five roof lanterns and sixty roof lights are filled with seven thousand eight hundred and seventy-three panes of glass. And so on.

'My father succeeded in May 1938,' said the Duke, sitting with his back to the window with the privileged view so that the illustrator could sketch him there, 'but he never really liked the house.' The war meant hard times for country houses as big as Chatsworth, because they were taken over by evacuees. Much the worst temporary tenants were troops. Five years of military occupation could wreak terrible havoc, but the Devonshires managed to get a girls' school from North Wales instead. They were much better behaved than soldiers and did little worse than hang irreverent placards around the necks of the classic nude statues in the gardens. They moved out again in 1946 but still meet at Chatsworth for reunions.

The Duke's youth was scarred by tragedy. His elder brother, the Marquess of Hartington and heir, of course, to the title and everything that went with it, was killed in 1944 during the war. Then a few years later his father, the 10th Duke, contracted a fatal illness. The law of the day was that, unless you found some adroit way of avoiding them, death duties were fixed at a crippling eighty per cent. At the time of his father's illness no such scheme had been concocted. When they did draw one up, part of the condition was that the exemption would only come into effect if the 10th Duke managed to live on for another five years. The wretched man failed by just four months. The law was later changed so that the liability was reduced on a sliding scale, but at the time the 11th Duke had to pay out the whole amount.

'We didn't panic,' he says. 'Luckily I had the benefit of brilliant legal advice, and also I was only thirty. Had I been fifty or even forty it might have been different, but I was young enough to have the strength to see it through.'

Hardwick Hall, another ancient family home, was sold to the National Trust. Land and farms went too. Great national institutions like the Victoria and Albert Museum made off with a number of masterpieces such as the Memling Triptych and the Holbein cartoon of Henry VIII. 'I minded that the most,' he says. But he derives a quiet satisfaction from the fact that the Rembrandt they had to lose has subsequently turned out not to be a Rembrandt after all. The two that he retained are not so doubtful. Books, tapestries and manuscripts also had to go, but the collection was so formidable that in the end, as the Duke puts it, laconically, 'We still had a nice lot left. It could have been much worse.'

At first he and the Duchess, their son and two daughters lived in what the Duke describes as 'a not very nice house in the village. It faced north and east.' When they opened Chatsworth to the public they had arranged the public tour in such a way that there was enough private accommodation to house the family if they needed it. 'So,' he says, 'in 1958 we took the decision to move back. It was a major job. We had to put in seventeen bathrooms.'

The arrangement seems to work well. It was blissfully quiet in the Duke's sitting-room, even though we had just driven through a car park jammed with cars and buses. Outdoors is the problem. Even their so-called private piece of garden is open to public view and since, in the spring, summer and autumn months, the punters don't have to be out till six, the amount of time the family can spend sitting around outside on their own and unobserved is sadly limited.

The next significant decision was taken in the 1970s. As befits a house with a history, nothing is done in too much of a hurry. The original death duties, for instance, were paid back over a total of seventeen years using real Fabius Cunctator tactics. They used to see how long the Revenue took to reply to each of their letters and always manage it so that their own replies were sent off in precisely twenty-four hours less than the Revenue's. That was how they could never – quite – be accused of delaying tactics.

'A Big House,' he says, in what I take to be a classic understatement, 'is a very great drain on an agricultural estate. We decided that it wasn't fair to ask the estate to go on bearing the burden of the house.' So in 1980 the Duke and the Marquess made over the house, contents and 1569 acres of garden, park and woods to a Chatsworth House Trust which pays a rent of £1 a year for the duration of its 99-year lease. The object of the Trust is 'the long term preservation of Chatsworth for the benefit of the public'. As the Duchess observes in her latest book it has great advantages for the Cavendish family. But, she adds, with just a touch of asperity, 'Perhaps I could be bold enough to say it is also an advantage for the house to be lived in and looked after by a family which invented it and is deeply bound to it by a multitude of ties which have grown up over nearly 450 years.' An advantage, she means, for the rest of us. It should also be emphasized that the Trust is heavily subsidized by the family who had to sell off yet more of their treasures, notably Poussin's *Holy Family*.

The Cavendishes have been at Chatsworth since the early years of the sixteenth century. They were originally a Suffolk family descended from Sir John, the Lord Chief Justice beheaded at Bury St Edmunds during the Peasants' Revolt. They came to Derbyshire when Sir William Cavendish married the formidable Bess of Hardwick, described by the present Duchess as the family's 'progenetrix'. It was solid, square and built round a courtyard.

After the 1688 revolution William Cavendish was created Duke of Devonshire for his services to William of Orange. ('My family have always been Whigs,' says the present Duke. He is now a member of the SDP.) A dukedom meant that a new house, less square and solid, more commensurate with ducal status, was required. Over twenty years Chatsworth was rebuilt on the old foundations, one front at a time. A formal garden was laid out and the great cascade installed. This is a wide staircase down which water tumbles from the hill above – except in the drought-like conditions of the summer of 1990. I love it, though Horace Walpole thought it an 'absurdity' on the deplorably prosaic grounds that it 'reduces the steps to be of no use at all'.

The 'new' Chatsworth was completed just before the 1st Duke died in 1707 and there were few significant changes until the time of the 4th Duke. He knocked down the stables and commissioned James Paine to build new ones, which now house the Chatsworth restaurant. The 4th Duke also commissioned Capability Brown to design a park. This involved removing the village of Edensor from its position smack in front of the house where it interfered with the view. It was rebuilt further away. Brown and the Duke also altered the course of the river and destroyed the formal garden in the interests of naturalness and romanticism. The effect is dramatic, but there is no denying that Brown was a bit of a vandal in his way.

The 6th Duke built the North Wing in the nineteenth century, but his finest achievements were in the garden. His head gardener was Joseph Paxton. He introduced rockeries, glasshouses and the massive 'Emperor' fountain whose jet can reach 280 feet on a calm day. It was built partly to impress the Tsar, who was coming to visit, but when the Tsar heard that it was higher than any fountain in the whole of Russia he developed a diplomatic illness and cancelled his trip. Paxton's crowning glory was a conservatory which covered three-quarters of an acre and was the model for the Crystal Palace which he built for the Great Exhibition of 1851. It fell into disrepair, however, and had to be demolished soon after the Great War. There is now a maze there instead.

The essential Chatsworth has not changed enormously since then, at least in appearance, though it would probably be fair to say that it has never been in better shape. That afternoon the deputy agent Roger Wardle gave us a lightning tour of the grounds. Up to the very top of Bess of Hardwick's hunting tower we went, standing under the flagpole from which the Arsenal Football Club flag had fluttered early in the year to mark the splendiferous celebrations of the Earl of Burlington's twenty-first. (The Earl is the son and heir of the Marquess.) Down to the Duke's Barn in Beeley, which has been given to the Royal School for the Deaf in Derby and turned into a residential field centre with new dormitories, audio-visual equipment and that recreational essential, a pool table. Over to Pilsley to the prosperous farm shop full of estate produce where I bought a free range duck and a box of the Duchess of Devonshire's chocolate chip biscuits.

'Seven hundred and fifty people live here,' says the Duke, talking about the sense of community which permeates the place. There is a bowling green and a cricket team, regular parties for the estate children, more than a hundred pensioners living rent free. The appearance of the cottages and farms is strictly controlled, so that there is a pleasing conformity to it all, an old-fashioned sense of everyone knowing his and her place. Feudal? Probably. But as the Duke says, 'It's certainly self interest. But I hope it's enlightened.' This Whiggish enlightenment even extends to the three hundred thousand or so people who come traipsing over his palatial dwelling every year. 'Oh,' he sighs, 'the murmur of voices, the smell of wet macintoshes. I really enjoy sitting by the open window and hearing the sound of children playing outside. Provided they're not too close. I don't think you'd feel comfortable living here and *not* sharing it. Even if I was really rich I wouldn't like not to have the public here.'

You could write books and books about Chatsworth. The present Duchess alone has already written two and is clearly just hitting her stride. I realize that I am nearing the end of this chapter and apart from our glass of sherry in the Duke's sitting room we have hardly been inside. Perhaps, however, there is another reason for this. I am not sure I really like much of the inside. Too strong a sense of gilt. Those pervasive ceilings by Laguerre, all pinkly sportive buttocks and nipples cavorting in curvaceous clouds and yards of diaphanous curtain material are just too much. I agree with the 6th Duke, who wrote of the State Dining Room, 'It was never dined in that I know of – the first room of this great unappropriated apartment, which consumes in useless display the best habitable part of the house.' You can have too much of showing off. I prefer such quirkinesses as the William Kent baby carriage, the Angela Connor busts of Betjeman and Macmillan. I'd rather have naked ladies by Lucien Freud than Sir Peter Lely. I am amused by the caique given to the 6th Duke by the Sultan of Turkey, by the Grinling Gibbons carving of woodcock and lace, above all by the superb van der vaart *trompe l'oeil* of a violin which hangs on the inner door to the music room and came from Devonshire House in Piccadilly, a London home demolished in 1924.

Perhaps there is too much showing off in Chatsworth, too much ostentation for comfort. Yet is has always been a house for showing off. The tradition of entertaining the public is as old as Chatsworth. Indeed the Estate office was first constructed as an inn for sightseers in 1775. In 1849 when the railway came to within three miles 80,000 people visited Chatsworth in a single summer. Five years earlier an article in *The Mirror of Literature and Amusement* explained, 'The Duke of Devonshire allows persons whatsoever to see the mansion and grounds every day in the year, Sundays not excepted from 10 in the morning till 5 in the afternoon. The humblest individual is not only shown the whole but the Duke has expressly ordered the waterworks to be played for everyone without exception. This is acting in the true spirit of great wealth and enlightened liberality; let us add, also, in the spirit of wisdom.'

This is a mite sycophantic, is must be said, and yet even if we do not go quite so far it is nevertheless very nice of the Duke to let us see his place. Nicer still that even if he didn't have to he would still feel an obligation. Oh all right, 'let us add, also, in the spirit of wisdom'. Or at least *enlightened* self-interest.

HARTLAND ABBEY

Hartland Abbey is the home of Betka Zamoyska's aunt. This is not the way most people would describe it, but as it is the reason Hartland is in the book it seemed the best way to begin. Betka is that comparative rarity, a journalist and writer who is also a Polish countess. She is the daughter of Count Andrzej, the sister of Count Zygmunt and the cousin of Count Zdzisz who is described in my *Debrett* as 'chef de famille in UK'. I was vaguely aware of all this, but I hadn't realized that Betka is just as grand, without the 'zeds', on the maternal side.

"You must go and see my aunt Sheila", she said decisively, when I told her that I was writing a book on historic houses, "She lives in this hidden valley in Devon. It's on the gulf stream and it runs all the way down to the sea."

Betka's mother, it transpired, is a Stucley, daughter of Sir Hugh, the 4th Baronet, aunt of the present Sir Hugh, sister of Sir Dennis, whose widow, Sheila, the Dowager Lady Stucley still lives in the Abbey. She, of course, is a Stucley only by marriage, being a Bampfylde by birth. Her father was Lord Poltimore, and there is still in the middle of Exmoor an excellent Poltimore Arms, one of the few remaining pubs to run its own cricket team. I hope I have got all this right. The details are of the sort which would give pleasure to that estimable genealogist and obituarist Hugh Montgomery-Massingberd. I don't however, pretend to his expertise.

Anyway, I filed Betka's information away and half forgot it. Hartland is remote from Richmond where I live. It's beyond Barnstaple and the only reason I could see for most people going there is to get shipwrecked. However, in the spring of 1990 I felt like a break and so did the rest of my family. We had a catalogue of National Trust holiday cottages, most of them in the West Country. They looked appealing, but on enquiry we found that most had been booked months earlier. The only one left was a farmhouse called Croyde Hoe, isolated on Baggy Point which reaches out into the Bristol Channel to the south of Lundy. If you walked across the field outside Croyde Hoe and if the weather was clear you could see right across Bideford Bay to the winking beam of the lighthouse at the end of Hartland Point. And there, tucked into her hidden valley just beyond it, was Betka's aunt.

I phoned her from the public call box by the caravan park down town. (The farmhouse had no phone, no electricity and I lit the gas lamps at night with a taper.)

'Could you come to lunch tomorrow?' she wanted to know. And would I like to bring my family, my wife.

'No, no,' I said, 'there are hordes of them.'

'Hordes of wives?' Her voice floated cheerily across the bay, clearly amused by the notion of a friend of Betka's practising polygamy in a National Trust farmhouse on Baggy Point.

The valley in which Hartland lies is so isolated that when they dissolved the monasteries it was overlooked until two years after everyone else. Although, as Lady Stucley put it, 'we could almost shake hands across the bay,' it was over an hour's drive from us to her. The narrow lanes round Croyde were simply not designed for all those Volkswagen Golfs and small Ford convertibles with surfboards on the roof, all driven maniacally fast by young men with shaved heads and reflecting dark glasses. Barnstaple, with its sprawling new estate, is a traffic jam. Then there is some smart new dual carriageway, but it soon returns to Chesterton's rolling road.

All along the north coast of Somerset and Devon, at least from Minehead where we had the first sightings of 'Lorna Doone' in Gothick script outside guest houses and tea shops, there is evidence of tourism. 'What exactly *is* a Devon clotted cream tea?' asked my elder son after a day of constant exposure to its advertisement. On our way to Hartland we passed two indications that Britain is well set to become the world's first national theme park. The first was something called 'Big Sheep'. This is sheep for tourists. You can try carding, spinning and weaving for yourself and buy sheep's milk fudge. We expressed scepticism, but at Hartland Abbey I found that Sir Hugh Stucley, his wife and daughters, had called there on their way down from their home at Affeton and pronounced it excellent. The second was the village of Clovelly. This is the archetypal picture postcard place with cottages built into the cliff and a cobbled main street fit only for donkeys. The Rous family, who own it, have built a visitor centre which would not seem out of place in Orlando, and charge a pound a head just for setting foot in it. Even in April, before the Easter holiday, the car park was almost full. Clovelly has been a tourist attraction for years, but even so . . .

Hartland Abbey is not like this at all. For a start it is virtually unsigned. We turned off the A39 shortly after Clovelly Cross, passed through the village of Hartland, famous, among other things, for its town band, which makes regular tours abroad. A little further on, through woodland awash with bluebells, we came on a gateway and drive. The sign made it plain that this was indeed an entrance to the Abbey. It was handpainted and although not actually uninviting in the sense that it did not say 'Private', 'Keep Out' and 'Trespassers will be Prosecuted', it did give the impression of intending to convey the sense of 'no'. We wound down the drive. A peacock screeched. There were two men at work in the garden. The tennis court had been abandoned. A fine old tree, which I later found was more than two hundred years old, lay shattered by the spring storms in the park immediately in front of the house. My family drove away to lunch in the pub at Hartland Quay, the Stucley's harbour a mile or so away, and I went in search of life. One of the gardeners directed me away from the front to the back door (he obviously recognized trade when he saw it), and I rang the bell feeling like Walter de la Mare's traveller.

'Tell them I came and no-one answered, That I kept my word', I felt like saying, since no one descended, let alone leaned over and looked into my eyes as I stood perplexed and still.

However, after I had rung a second time I heard footsteps and the door was opened by a woman, stoutish and clearly not Lady Stucley. Evidently she hadn't known whether it was the front door bell or the back, and there was a further moment of confusion because seeing me clutching my clipboard she assumed, understandably, that I was canvassing or conducting some sort of survey.

All was explained, however, and she led me along what seemed interminable rather cold and dark corridors before ushering me into a surprisingly warm and friendly library where a woman who plainly *was* Lady Stucley was phoning a man about a television set. The room is not usually on show, and it's one of the few remaining bits of the original Abbey. Lady Stucley said I was right to find it friendly. Everyone said the same. It had a sense of peace which, she was sure, had a lot to do with its ancient monastic history.

From the windows you could see across the park to an old look-out on the hillside. The sea is immediately beyond.

To the left of the look-out is St Nectan's Church, Stoke. This is the Hartland parish church and has the highest tower in all Devon. When the Abbey was consecrated by Bishop Bartholomew of Exeter in 1160 the monks were supposed to serve the church, named after one of those Devonian martyrs whose fame, alas, seldom seems to extend beyond the county. Local martyr. The natives apparently killed him for his sheep rather than his beliefs. The monks were of the regular order of St Augustine of Hippo. 'There used to be a secret passage from the house up to the church,' said Lady Stucley pouring me a sherry, 'but my father-in-law had it blocked up.' The church is large for the community it serves, but between eighty and a hundred people worship there every Sunday and the choir is thirty-five strong. When the Abbey is open to the public the Church Council are responsible for afternoon tea. Sir Allen Lane, the founder of Penguin Books, is a local man and is buried and commemorated at St Nectan's.

'I've been here since 1932,' said Lady Stucley. 'First of all in the cottage, and then here since 1934. In the war it was taken over first by a school, Highgate Junior, I think, and then by a girls' finishing school called The Monkey Club.' The Monkey Club seem to have been rather better tenants than Highgate Junior. 'Then six years

ago,' she continued, 'we were faced with capital transfer tax and couldn't cope with it' so we became a "Heritage House". We open on Easter Sunday, Bank Holidays and then every Wednesday and Sunday afternoon from mid July to mid September.' They have around four thousand visitors a year.

Its been a private house since its rather belated dissolution in 1539. It was the last monastic house in England to go. The reason, according to legend at least, is that it's so remote and secluded that it simply got overlooked. When it had been dissolved and the monks had gone, Henry VIII gave it to his wine steward at Hampton Court, a man called William Abbott.

Since then the fortunes of the house have been largely determined by the advantageous marriages of three heiresses. The first, Catherine Abbot, married Nicholas Luttrell of Dunster Castle up the coast near Minehead, so the Abbey became a Luttrell House for a hundred years; then heiress number two, Mary Luttrell, married Paul Orchard from Kilkhampton. He was a customs officer and it was he who made the first serious alterations to the Abbey, signing his work with a stone in the south wall which says simply 'P.O. & M 1705'. His son went a lot further fifty years later. He razed the Great Hall and the chapel to the ground and sliced the top floor off the east side of the main building. Then he replaced this with three big reception rooms and bedrooms, all in Strawberry Hill Gothick. The exterior of the house remains much the same today. The third heiress, Anne Orchard, married a Mr Buck from Bideford. Later the family became Stucley-Bucks and then, when the baronetcy was conferred in Disraeli's premiership, the Buck half of the name disappeared altogether.

It's one of those families and one of those houses that feels as if it is always on the fringe of great events but never quite centre stage. There used to be a first edition of *Paradise Regained* on Lady Stucley's shelves. It was inscribed to 'My dear friend Lewis' from Milton himself. It had to be sold, alas. 'I hated letting that go,' says Lady Stucley. Sir Lewis escorted Sir Walter Raleigh to the scaffold and his account of it is in the document collection. Also at Hartland is Parson Jack Russell's hunting gear. Russell, the man who gave his name to the doggy little terrier the Kennel Club won't recognize as a breed, was a friend of the Poltimore family, and one of his favourite days' hunting was at Hartland. Somehow the combination of a lost *Paradise Regained* and Jack Russell's whip and boots is typical of the house. Full of extraordinary things but low on order and logic; full, therefore, of curious and very English surprises. Notice the Kneller in the Little Dining Room. It is of Dr William Stukeley, the early eighteenth-century archaeologist who was responsible for saving Stonehenge, Avebury and Hadrian's Wall for the nation. Even more unexpected is the silver-mounted wheelbarrow and spade in the Inner Hall. It was presented in 1864 to Florence, Lady Poltimore, on the opening of the Devon and Somerset Railway which ran from Taunton to Barnstaple. You see what I mean.

'There was no electric light when we moved in,' said Lady Stucley, 'no proper heating and a great many rats.' It's still far from warm. The three great reception rooms at the north, built by the younger Paul Orchard and Victorianized by Sir George Stucley with help from Sir George Gilbert Scott, are never used in winter and not exactly cosy in summer. There's a drawing-room, billiard room and dining-room, and Lady Stucley took me through them at a briskish clip after lunch in her small private dining-room upstairs – saddle of lamb carved by her son, Sir Hugh, the first of the season's rhubarb, clotted cream and cider.

The rooms are undeniably grand. The linenfold panelling is copied from the House of Lords. The stone of the fireplace in the billiard room was brought to Hartland Quay from Malta in Sir George Stucley's yacht. Sir George sounds rather a card. So does the Lewis Buck whose Victorian campaign song in the nineteenth-century North Devon election went to the tune of 'The House that Jack built.' It ran: 'Buck's the dog/that will worry the cat/beat Buller the rat/and guard the corn/that lies in the house the farmer built.' And Lady Stucley herself has a certain family cardishness. The unusual Heath Robinson expanding dining table, for instance, is not a family heirloom but a little something she picked up years ago for a tenner. Sotheby's got quite excited when they came down to do a valuation, but Lady Stucley is sensible about it. 'Five children, nineteen grandchildren and five great-grandchildren,' she points out. That's a potential twenty-nine for lunch, not counting spouses.

The chief glory of the house is the document collection. There is a twelfth-century deposition from a local farmer swearing by St Nectan's bones that he will stop kidnapping and assaulting the King's messengers. There are royal seals, starting with one of Edward IV's, continuing with three of Henry VIII's confirming the sale of the Abbey to Mr Abbott and including others from Elizabeth I, both Charleses, Queen Anne, the first four Georges and William IV. In all there are several thousand bits and pieces. And, in typical Hartland Abbey style, this extraordinary treasure trove lay hidden in a chest in the cellar until the late Sir Dennis and his daughter Margaret discovered it by chance in 1952.

Which, in a way, brings us back to the beginning. For Sir Dennis's daughter Margaret, like Lady Stucley, is, of course, Betka Zamoyska's aunt, and if it hadn't been for Betka I wouldn't have known that Hartland existed. Then I should have overlooked it as Thomas Cromwell's men so nearly did in the sixteenth century when it almost became the only monastery in England not to be dissolved.

And I should have been sorry.

WESTON PARK

The last time the illustrator and I went to a point-to-point it rained. We were reporting it for *Punch* and the illustrator ended up taking refuge in the back of someone's Range Rover while I got sprayed with mud from the swirling wheels of stuck stockbroker Mercedes. That was a Home Counties affair with a slightly ersatz feel of countryside. Not quite the real thing.

This time we were at the 'Point-to-point steeplechases' of the West Shropshire Hunt, held in the grounds of Weston Park 'by kind permission of the Earl of Bradford'. This was an altogether more bucolic affair, as you would expect from a place which has a telephone exchange called 'Weston-under-Lizard'. It's about half an hour's drive from Stafford. The names of the adjacent hunts give you some idea of where we are: the Albrighton, the Cheshire Forest, the Flint and Denbigh, the Holecombe, the Meynell and South Staffs, the North Shropshire, the North Staffs, Sir William Watkin Wynns, the Tanatside, the South Shropshire. The first race was at 12.30 and was 'The B and D Steel Group West Shropshire Hunt Members Race for Lightweights and Heavyweights'. It was over three miles, and T. Jones, the Oswestry saddlers, had kindly donated a prize to be given to the owner of the winning horse. The horses had names just like real race horses – Mister Kilo, Nudge Nudge, Red Wharf Bay, Scally's Lay – but somehow gave the impression, to the layman like me, that they were a class short. Under 'form', for instance, the last named was dismissed with 'No known assessable form over fences or hurdles'. Others were 'strong finisher, inconsistent', 'promising youngster, has a turn of foot' and 'takes a few chances'.

Barbour and binocular; Land Rover and labrador; navy blue trilbies with leather thongs; international rugby relayed on screens by the Tote; rubbery hot dogs and thick sweet instant coffee; a voice over the Tannoy saying 'All other horses are disqualified, so would all other owners return their rosettes and prize money to the secretary's tent'; hairy farmers off small white hill farms in mid-Wales; horsey aunts in Blandings house parties. This is the sort of thing that goes on, by his kind permission, in the Earl of Bradford's garden.

I didn't see the Earl that day, though he could have been mingling with the crowd. I had first met him some months earlier at a board meeting of 'Royal Britain', a doomed monarchical Madame Tussaud's operation, master-minded by our mutual

friend Gyles Brandreth, the after-dinner speaker and gamester. Lord Bradford had been wheeled in to this enterprise on account, I think, of his title and his catering. Not only is he Richard Thomas Orlando Bridgeman, 7th Earl, he is also the owner of Porters Restaurant in Covent Garden and the compiler of two books, *My Private Parts and the Stuffed Parrot* and The *Eccentric Cookbook*. A jovial, bearded, youngish (born 1947), man of parts.

He inherited Weston Park on the death of his father in 1981. His family and what he describes as his 'forebears' have been there since the twelfth century. I am not one hundred per cent clear about the exact relationship between the present Earl and Rainald de Balgiole, owner of Weston at the time of Domesday in the 1080s. Rainald was sheriff to Roger de Montgomery, the Earl of Shrewsbury, and his family seem to have taken the name of the place as their own because the 'de Westons' were in residence until 1350. The male line died out then and the property descended through the female line to Adam de Peshall who was succeeded by his son-in-law Sir Richard de Mytton, who begat several generations of Weston-owning Myttons until an only daughter called Elizabeth married Sir Thomas Wilbraham, a Cheshire baronet. At the time of her marriage in 1651 Elizabeth was only ninteen years old, but she turned out to be the make of the modern pile, which dates, in effect, from 1671 and replaced the much more modest medieval manor house.

I use the word pile advisedly, not just because it is big and brick but because on the day of the West Shrops point-to-point it had a closed and shuttered look which was, frankly, a little bleak. I would have liked to see a procession of sprigs and sprogs of the aristocracy issuing forth from french windows in creamy jodhpurs; a butler or two should, in an ideal world, have been shimmying out from under the portico at the east front bearing a salver with glasses of hot negus. But no. For when he succeeded to the title the present Earl moved out of the great house and down the road with his wife Joanne and their sons Alexander (aka Viscount Newport), Henry and Benjamin. So although, as he says, they do 'try to convey the impression of Weston Park very much as being a well equipped family home', in a sense this is an illusion. It is still a family home, but the family does not live there. Instead you yourselves may move in with no fewer than fourteen and no more than thirty-five friends and colleagues and play – at a price – at being Lord or Lady of the Manor. There are twenty bedrooms sleeping up to thirty-six guests, all with direct dial telephones. Oh, and a new conference room seating sixty. The food, as you would expect from an Earl with his reputation in catering, is given appropriate weight. For a 'Weston Park Gourmet House Party', he proposes a terrine of duck and duck livers with cranberry sauce, a mousse of smoked trout and chives with a tomato and basil sauce, a pear and rum sorbet, a lamb fillet in Madeira sauce served with onion marmalade, a black-berry and lemon syllabub, coffee and home-made *petits fours*. To accompany this you are recommended Bodenham Seyve Villard 1984, Tinto Olarra reserva 1976, Muscat de Beaumes de Venise, and Port, Brandy and Liqueurs. Next morning you will further be encouraged to have a traditional English breakfast which, claims the Earl, will 'satisfy even the greatest trencherman'.

This sounds like killer hospitality. After it, one assumes, the average business-man will stumble into the conference room for a quiet kip while the guest lecturer talks statistics and shows slides. For those who really want a coronary, however, there are various sporting activities on offer in the thousand acres of Capability Brown park. Clay pigeon shooting, archery, horse riding, fishing, pheasant shooting, hovercraft driving, parascending, ballooning ('Please note. Should it be too windy to fly when the crew arrive, the fee has to be paid in full.'), and even, wait for it, 'Task Force Military Game – prices on application'.

I know that during the last war the Special Operations Executive took over Lord Montagu's estate at Beaulieu and trained their agents there, but unless Lord Bradford has a contract with the eighth Armoured Brigade this does seem a tiny bit peculiar. As if all this eating, drinking and martial activity wasn't enough, Lord Bradford also has a suggested list of nocturnal activities in the house: casino evenings, a Black Country night out, a musical cabaret, a plain after-dinner speaker or a 'murder evening'. The paying guest at Weston does not just get a room with a view but a room with a venue. 'The Midlands' Finest' in the words of the brochure.

I would not like to be thought to be denigrating Lord Bradford's showmanship and commercial acumen. The house that Lady Wilbraham built is a stately edifice, and her descendants and his ancestors have made it statelier yet, as well as filling it with enough fine pictures and *objets d'art* to stir the appetite of the most sated business guest.

The Wilbraham dynasty was short-lived because they had three daughters. Mary, the heiress, married a Richard Newport who became 2nd Earl of Bradford, though this title died out with his son Thomas, the 4th Earl, who fell off his horse and never fully recovered. His nephew, Sir Orlando Bridgeman, succeeded. His son, Henry, became the 1st Baron Bradford and the baron's son Orlando became the 1st Earl of Bradford in 1815. The 1st Earl, I suppose I should say, in the second creation. From then on, I am relieved to say, the house and the Earldom have passed down in simple orderly form from one elder son to another.

Over the centuries the family has acquired more than its fair share of Old Masters. Here, in the breakfast room, for instance, is Holbein's picture of Sir George Carew, who went down with the *Mary Rose* in 1545 and who, as we have seen, is commemorated in the little museum at the old Carew family home at Bickleigh Castle. Other pictures in the breakfast room include a Gainsborough of Viscountess Torrington (Earl Orlando married Lucy Byng, Viscount Torrington's daughter in the eighteenth century). There is also Carlo Maratta's copy of Van Dyck's triple portrait of Charles I, a Cornelius Johnson of the Bishop of Chester, Dr John Bridgeman, whose son Orlando was the 1st Baronet. I am not particularly fond of the portrait of Lady Diana Russell by Paul Van Somer (like so many child portraits it looks more like an adult dwarf than a recognizable child), but it is good to find her teething stick preserved in a glass case underneath.

As always, it is small oddities such as this which intrigue and amuse me more than the Gobelins in the Tapestry Room or even the austere Constable of the Rev. George Bridgeman. I prefer the titles of the books on the secret doors in the library (*The Library of Useless Knowledge, How to Stop a Gap* and the *American Peerage*). The stuffed parrot is good too. It is a yellow parrot, alive when Benjamin Disraeli presented it to the 3rd Countess. Both Disraeli and the Countess thought it was a cock, but in 1903, more than twenty years after Disraeli's death, the parrot laid an egg. It went on laying eggs for twenty-three days, and on the twenty-fourth it died.

There must be some sort of moral in this, though it is difficult to be sure what. Disraeli and Selina, the Countess, conducted a correspondence which lasted for eight years, and eleven hundred of the Prime Ministers letters are preserved at Weston. Letter writing in those days was often the art of the insconsequential. 'I am sorry to write you such a scribbling letter,' he said once on a funereally black-bordered, post-Albertian missive from Windsor Castle, 'but I have only a moment. I go this morning to Longleat. The messenger who meets me at Slough will I hope bring me a letter from you: it seems a long time since I received one.' And thus, plaintive, he signed himself, 'Your affectionate, D.' In the same room, the West Marble Hall, there is another note, this time from King Charles II to Sir Orlando Bridgeman. He is asking him to return the Great Seal of England.

Like all the best English houses, Weston is full of such parenthetical nuggets of English history. Did you know, for instance, that another Orlando Bridgeman was the one and only witness of the marriage between the Prince Regent and Mrs Fitzherbert? There's immortality for you: an indelible footnote in the History of England. Modern Weston, 'The Midlands' Finest Venue', might yet provide such minutiae in the margins of history, for who knows what deals may be wheeled during the trencherman's breakfast at a business seminar or conference launch? Yet there is no denying that something of the old flavour has gone.

At Culzean Castle shortly after the point-to-point I bumped into a man who had been agent to the present Earl's father. He remembered Gerald Michael Orlando Bridgeman with an almost dewy-eyed nostalgia. The 6th Earl was much vexed by the rabbits. On one occasion he spotted one through a ground-floor window. It was munching his grass with a desultory contempt. His Lordship rang for his butler and complained. Seconds later there was a shot and the butler reappeared with a smoking twelve-bore and a dead rabbit which looked suspiciously as if it had just been removed from the deep-freeze.

'No rabbits in the park, my Lord,' said the artful butler.

Later on I repeated the tale to the latest Earl, Richard the Caterer. He chuckled. 'No rabbits in the park, my Lord,' he repeated.

It was clearly an old story. It couldn't happen now, and while in a manner of speaking that is a matter of pride and satisfaction, it is also, to me, a matter of regret.

No rabbits in the park, no family in the house. The commercial imperative rules, and there are company directors in the boudoir, account executives in the four-poster; 'all prices are exclusive of staff gratuities'; and John Betjeman, had he lived to see the day, would have made it rhyme in caustic verse. It would have been a cheap shot, however, because without Lord Bradford's very modern business sense and flair Weston Park would be crumbling away. As it is, the old house liveth . . . though I wonder what Lady Wilbraham would have thought.

STYLES

Bodger, the butler, met us at the quayside. I had known his kinsman, Eric, vaguely, at Balliol and there was a definite physical resemblance as he laid the last of the lobster-pots in the stern of the little boat, wiped his hands on his blue dungarees, and removed his clay pipe in order to articulate a curt, 'You'll be the writer chappie and the man who paints!?'

'That is us,' I said, falling in with Bodger's quaint sentence construction.

'His Serene Highness be expecting you,' he said and turned towards he island, which lay no more than a few hundred yards offshore. At low tide you could walk across on the 'Dwarf's Causeway', but our train had left us at high tide and the causeway was under water. The island, shrouded in heat-haze, seemed far further off than it really was. It actually stands only eight hundred yards off shore but that day, an hour or so short of lunch, it looked, shimmering, silver and ethereal, as distant as Atlantis.

We had come, the illustrator and I, on what had once upon a time been the Cornish Riviera Express from Paddington but was now a High Speed Train with designer sandwiches and tea made from the leaf in the buffet. Alighting at Dawlish Warren, just beyond Exeter, we had then taken a taxi the three miles to the Margrave of Stollen and Windbutel's private harbour, otherwise known as Creamery Quay. We had been asked to spend the weekend on the Island of Styles, which had been the romantic private domain of the Bingen family ever since George III had given it to the present Margrave's ancestor Klaus von und zu Bingen, 10th Margrave of Stollen und Windbutel, in 1773. One story had it that George's present was the result of Klaus, one of the pre-eminent physicians of his day, having cured one of the monarch's periodic fits of lunacy; another, more plausibly, held that the island had been donated during a period of dementia. Klaus had been a lover of Fanny Burney's and lived in a one-room house on the riverside at Kew. He was obsessed by water.

The present Margrave, the 17th is a friend of my friend Philip Howard, the brilliant half-blind, half-Greek, Literary Editor of *The Times*. He served in the Royal Scots Greys when Howard was doing national service with the Black Watch in Berlin. They met when the two regiments were dancing sixteensomes against each other. One or other had been 'birled' out of a first-floor window, an event leading to a broken

collar-bone and a lifelong friendship. Philip engineered the invitation over lunch at the Garrick.

There has been a dwelling on Styles since the ninth century, when Saint God-wotte lived here in a stone bothy, part of whose walls have been incorporated into the present house. So have the remains of the subsequent Benedictine Abbey, which was partially destroyed at the Dissolution of the Monasteries when the island passed to Sir Roger de Totnes, Keeper of the King's Condiments. The de Totnes family eventually went into exile in the mid eighteenth century when their Jacobite plottings were discovered. Sir Roy de Totnes, his wife and five children, all fled to France in a schooner, and the island remained uninhabited until the arrival of Klaus in 1773.

It was his son Ferdinand, the 11th Margrave, who was largely responsible for building the present house. There is nothing else quite like it in the British Isles, for it is in all essential respects an exact copy of a Bavarian castle. The timbers and the stone were all shipped from the Bingen estates in Koblenz and Niederbayern. German architects were brought in to design the soaring turrets, battlements and the wrought-iron weather-vanes; German muralists painted the gory hunting scenes on the stucco in the courtyard; herds of German deer were mown down to provide the antlers which festoon the exterior walls.

Inside, the Germanic sense has been leavened by generations of English wives. Klaus himself had taken a child bride from Mauritius, but she, Claudia, a stunning beauty judging by the exquisite little portrait by Kynphausen in the Beige Drawing Room, was the last non-English Bingen bride. Every Margravine of Stollen and Windbutel since the late eighteenth century had been of English or Scottish lineage, so that despite their German titles the Bingens have become more British than the British – though their dark good looks still hark back to the influence of the beautiful Mauritian 10th Margravine.

Her Serene Highness, Lady Araminta, the present Margravine, is a distant kinswoman of the Duke of Buccleuch. She and her children, Damian, Alexander, Polly, Sam, Tarquin and Emma were already down on Drake's Lawn overlooking the sea. It was here that a young Totnes first spotted the sails of the Spanish Armada in 1588. The family lit a beacon on the very spot and the message literally flashed across Britain to Queen Elizabeth herself. Nowadays the lawn is used for croquet and picnics. Right on the clifftop there is an octagonal gazebo designed by Sir Charles Barry. In it Prince Albert, a close friend of the Bingen family, made sketches for a revolutionary pair of binoculars containing tinted glass so that they could be used while looking into the sun. Here too he composed a sonnet for the house which is on a wall in the summer-house, handstitched on a sampler by Constance, eldest daughter of the 14th Margrave. It's not very good.

The family was drinking Pimm's Number Six from silver half-pint tankards. The

Margrave introduced them all rather solemnly and formally. They ranged in age from late twenties to twelve-year-old Emma, a dimpled, tomboyish afterthought. Below us the waves plopped plangently on the pebbles; out to sea I could just make out the Wizard's Light and the outline of an empty super tanker heading for the Gulf. The mew of the gulls, the clink of floating ice against heavy eighteenth-century German silver; the languid drawl of English aristocratic small talk; it was all quite idyllic.

"Any relation of Sir Lionel? . . . I hear you review for funny old Philip . . . Which college was that? . . . Never met the fellow I'm sorry to say . . . The pater put that stained-glass window in after my uncle was killed in Burma . . . an absolute four letter man, black sheep of the family and all that . . . he drank for Devon . . . Quelle disaster . . . Emma darling, could you run and ask Bodger to bring some more ice?"

There were gull's eggs with celery salt and smoked salmon and crusty brown bread baked that morning by Mrs Bodger and butter from the tiny herd of Styles cattle who could be seen grazing on Raleigh's Sward beyond the west wing. And there was cold sea-trout caught by the Margrave the previous day and new potatoes and mint and tiny young broad beans all from the great walled garden erected as part of the landscaping carried out in the nineteenth century by the now forgotten 'Competence Fry', the hunchback protégé of Isambard Kingdom Brunel. And that was followed by fresh raspberries and nectarines from the greenhouses and cream from the cows and to drink with it there was a delicate flowery Alsatian Gewurztraminer from a friend's vineyard. And to end there was a Jamaican cigar from another friend who was the Custos Rotulorum somewhere in the Blue Mountains. I felt like the mole in *The Wind in the Willows*, incapable of anything but holding up my paws and exclaiming, 'O my! O my! O my!'

There is a natural rock pool at the foot of the cliffs and a long while after the last of the lunch we ambled down there just as Victoria and Albert had done almost a hundred and fifty years before. 'Albert bathed,' wrote the Queen. 'The water cold despite the sun which shone all day. The dear Margrave was in great good humour and raced Albert from one end to another winning every time and causing poor Albert some distress.' This time there was no racing though a beach ball was produced and some desultory attempts were made at water polo. The illustrator and I did not excel.

The shadows were lengthening by the time we climbed back to the old *Schloss*. An oddity of the house is that it has never had a name other than that of the island itself. It is neither 'Castle', 'House' nor even 'Abbey', just 'Styles'. Alastair had some phone calls to make connected with the computer company of which he is chairman, so he begged to be excused while Lady Araminta gave us what he referred to as "the two and sixpenny tour".

The Long Gallery is very long, the Beige Drawing Room very beige, the Gun

Room full of guns and the Billiard Room of cues and balls and a great slab of felt covered Burroughs and Watts. In these respects it resembles many other historic English country houses. Its Germanic exterior finds surprisingly few echoes indoors. It has a light, chintzy, very ENGLISH feel. There were flowers everywhere, especially huge arrangements of sweet peas filling every room with their scent. And everywhere too there was evidence of family life – the occasional labrador, tongue lolling with the heat, a fat Siamese cat sprawled in front of the four-door oil-fired Aga, a *Wisden Cricketer's Almanack* open in the study alongside the latest P. D. James, signed photographs of royalty and even, amusingly, one of Philip Howard in cricket togs.

There are, of course, family portraits by Kneller, Reynolds, Sargent and the rest. But some are more modern and less orthodox. Lady Araminta is still, in her early fifties, a strikingly fine-looking woman. The Lucien Freud portrait of her was done some thirty years ago and yet I still found it unnerving to have it pointed out by her. Like most of Freud's studies of the female form it strikes one as being almost too candid. Lady Araminta's comments were somehow typical. 'That sofa was frightfully uncomfortable and I was covered in goose pimples. It was February and there were nothing but power cuts. Brrr.'

There is also a very peculiar portrait of the present Margrave by Francis Bacon.

Two other highly distinctive peculiarities. Practically every room in the house had the most spectacular sea views. The windows are often enormous and those opening on to the south terrace from the Long Gallery stretch from the floor almost to the ceiling. The only great house that I know with comparable views is Culzean in Ayrshire, but Culzean not being on an island doesn't have the all-round vistas of Styles. Nor, of course, does it have a Globe.

This extraordinary room is not part of the house proper but was built on top of the great clocktower which apes Barry's Big Ben and which stands in the middle of the lawn outside the Palladian stable block. There isn't a single straight line in it and it has no sensible function other than to act as a look-out or viewing station. On a clear day, they say, you can see all the way to Dunkery Beacon. It is a wonderful piece of Victorian madness.

The Bingens are now a German family only in name, and the eccentric memorabilia dotted about the house are as English, well British, as the Bingens themselves have become: Lord Byron's cricket bat; Benjamin Jowett's mortar-board; a pair of roller-skates reputed to have belonged to W. G. Grace; an extravagantly passionate collection of letters from Virginia Woolf to Constance Bingen, the suffragette; a recipe for Arnold Bennett omelette written in the author's own hand; the steam-powered fire-engine which so enchanted Victoria and Albert on their visit; the sixteenth Margrave's Second World War medals and the fifteenth Margrave's First – he won an MC on the Somme. There is even a stuffed pig in the hall. His name was

Fritz and he was a famous Styles fixture in the 1890s, a particular pet of Alastair's great-grandmother who fed him on Turkish Delight and *marrons glacés*. He liked swimming.

After dinner in the pillared dining-room, windows open so that we could hear the sea outside, we played an arcane form of Styles' slosh at the billiard table, and gossiped, and drank Hine cognac far into the night. Next day we breakfasted late and there were no Sunday papers but we strolled round the island – which took about an hour – and played a little croquet and drank a little Pimms and then suddenly almost before we realized it Bodger was at the jetty with the boat and it was time to return on the 4.50 to Paddington.

As we sailed away to the mainland the family gathered on the quayside to wave us goodbye. The Margrave had brought down a very old wind-up gramophone with a horn to serenade our departure. I can hear the crackling tune wafting across the water from that enchanted island even as I write.

Alastair had chosen his Master's voice:
The Stately Homes of England.
Tho' rather in the lurch,
Provide a lot of chances
For Psychical Research –
There's the ghost of a crazy younger son
Who murder'd in Thirteen Fifty-One,
An extremely rowdy Nun
Who resented it
And people who come to call
Meet her in the hall.

Styles is reputed to have not a rowdy nun ghost but a randy monk ghost. Only ladies ever see him. At least that was what the Margrave told me.

I mentioned it to our mutual friend the Literary Editor later over lunch, but he only smirked and said, 'If you believe that you'll believe anything.' He may be right. I am essentially very credulous. All the same I can't help feeling that if there isn't such a ghost then someone should invent him *quam celerrime*. But then I feel like that about a lot of people.

And places.

SANDFORD ORCAS MANOR

When I was at school at Sherborne in Dorset Sir Hubert Medlycott of Sandford Orcas Manor was the chairman of governors. He was very very old and frail, with a quavering, much imitated voice and the absolute lack of self-consciousness enjoyed only by those under five or over eighty. I remember him one year at one of the great ritual services in Sherborne Abbey – Commem or the Christmas Carols – when he had to read a lesson from the Old Testament. He shuffled up to the lectern, blinked a few times at the good book on the brass eagle, then produced his own smaller bible and placed it on the floor. A shaft of sunlight beamed down and illuminated the pages. Then he knelt and read.

The present owner of Sandford Orcas Manor, Sir Hubert's grandson, Sir Mervyn, the 8th Baronet, remembers staying with his grandfather as a child and being shown round Sherborne School 'as if it was his own personal domain'. In those days the Manor was served by a full staff of servants, a thriving community in its own right, but today Sir Mervyn, a bachelor, lives there on his own, supported only by a couple who come in to help. When I wrote suggesting a visit he replied courteously that he doubted whether the house had enough going on to interest me. 'Most of the time except public opening days,' he said, 'it leads a rather somnolent existence, with not much happening at all.'

He did, however, offer a suggestion. 'On July 8th I shall be having in the garden here, weather permitting, the village fête.'

I found the idea of Sir Mervyn Medlycott at the Sandford Orcas village fête irresistible, especially in view of his other mild caveat. On the day itself, he warned, 'I doubt whether I could give very much of my time, as I am on the organizing committee and am also running the "White Elephant" stall.'

In the end, alas, weather did not permit. It was one of those irritatingly iffy days, uncharacteristic of a, for the most part, freakishly sun-saturated summer. The illustrator and I set out early by train from Waterloo and it was grey all the way through Woking, Basingstoke, Andover, Salisbury and Templecombe. How often in grey suit and stiff white detachable collar I had made that glum journey to school. Sherborne

is a pretty, even beautiful town but I cannot walk about it without apprehension. The ghost of the headmaster in gown and mortar board is always there asking why I am not wearing my straw boater, why my jacket is undone, why my shoes aren't polished. I am still fearful of committing beatable offences without realizing it. Even a pint of Badger Ale in the Half Moon Hotel as we waited for a taxi to take us to Sandford Orcas induced a frisson of guilt. After all, this is what my friend Nigel Dempster was expelled for all those years ago. Well, this and girls.

The village of Sandford Orcas *nestles*. The picture postcard word is apt for once. Cheapened by cliché, it is still the only word that will do: 'late Middle English, to lodge or settle as in a nest . . . to lie half hidden or embedded in some place or thing . . . snuggle, settle or cuddle closely.' This is what Sandford Orcas does. Lord David Cecil once wrote: 'Sandford Orcas is a "buried" house; buried in the countryside, buried in the past.' Even more so in summer when the banks are dense with green and the white froth of Queen Anne's Lace. You feel as if you have tunnelled to reach it and when you are there the world feels literally a world outside.

We were early so we went to the pub. The pub was a reminder of what anyone who has ever read a classic English whodunnit (much less tried to write one) knows by instinct. The English village is seldom as idyllic as it looks. The pub is called the Mitre. It does proper food and is run by a couple called Phil and Brenda. The menu on our visit included shark. We had a pint of prawns apiece with home-made garlic mayonnaise and drank draught cider with it.

You will have guessed by now that Phil and Brenda are not indigenous Sandford Orcadians. They have come from Redhill in Surrey, where Phil had a garage. When I asked him if he knew whether or not the fête had been cancelled on account of the weather he gave me a look which said, 'Don't ask me, sunshine, nobody tells me anything.' 'We're pariahs,' he said. The story was straight from the new-look version of Britain's most popular radio soap with its emphasis on social realism and all that. Phil had applied for planning permission to put a bungalow in the field next to his pub. Fine uproar all round of the sort which the Hampshire Brigadiers produced when Nicholas Ridley approved a new town at Foxley Wood. However, when Phil's application was duly and predictably turned down he retaliated by putting pigs into the field instead. More local uproar. People come from as far as Bournemouth to have prawns and shark at the Mitre, but most of the village folk won't set foot in the place. Not that Phil cares. Last time they came in they spent two hours nursing half-pints of bitter and packets of crisps. Dramas like this are being played out all over England whenever townees move in and interlope, thus disturbing the status quo so jealously preserved by generation upon generation of Medlycotts at the Manor.

Not that Sir Mervyn seemed to be aware of the drama at the pub. We finally caught up with him in the village hall otherwise known as the Sandford Orcas

Snooker and Billiard Club. He was quite agitated by our arrival. 'I phoned,' he said, 'but you'd already left.' Yeovilton, the local Royal Naval Air Station had, incorrectly, forecast rain, and the fête organizing committee had decided to opt for the wet weather plan. Everything had been transferred from the manor lawn to the hall. Sir Mervyn was terribly sorry about it, not least because he had done a tremendous job on his tractor mower eliminating the thistles.

He was easy to pick out despite the throng because he is extremely tall. Grey, spectacled, diffident, just the wrong side of forty, he loomed over the villagers like a giant river bird. The white elephants on his stall seemed to consist almost entirely of glasses, cups and saucers, not in very good nick. 'Big things ten p,' he said, 'Small things five p.' I was half tempted by a book called *The Complete Guide to Canadian Cookery* and another entitled *No Place for Ponies*. There were cream teas for £1.20 and in a muddy field behind the hall you could shy coconuts or try to kill a toy rat. 'The village ratcatcher proudly presents "Kill the Rat," a sophisticated game of skill and co-ordination.' Wellie hurling, lucky dips, guess the weight of the pig, win a bunch of sweet peas, roll up, roll up. All the fun of the fête. 'Mervyn,' said an official fête organizing lady, 'Can I borrow you to draw the raffle?' Mervyn stalked off obediently.

Despite the family connection he was not educated at Sherborne but at Milton Abbey. ('A school for duffers,' he says disarmingly, 'But they didn't tell me till later.') A genealogist by trade, he is President and founder – in 1975 – of the Somerset and Dorset Family History Society. Living in the Manor and showing people round himself therefore absorbs him. There were more than 2,500 visitors last year. More, he says, than either he or the house can really cope with. It is a small house by manorial standards, and although it is open to the public, the operation is conducted utterly without commercialism, let alone vulgarity. He is emphatically not in showbusiness. Nor really in business at all.

Alec Clifton-Taylor in a book called *Buildings of Delight,* described the house as 'a perfect example of its type and period'. This is an expert view, though he was wrong in dating the building from 1535. Sir Mervyn says it was built about fifteen years later in 1550, the year that Edward VI 'of pious memory' granted a charter to Sherborne School. It reminds me mildly of school, perhaps because like the core of Sherborne it is built from lovely light gold Ham stone, quarried from the hill beyond Yeovil where my mother's family came from. It's the warmest stone in the world and despite my ambivalent views about school I love it.

We had tired of the fête before Sir Mervyn and left as we heard the command 'Now we'll move on to the Treasure Hunt'. We paused in the church where there is a tablet saying, 'I pray you remember before God Hubert James Medlycott of Ven Milborne Port and the Manor House Sandford Orcas Bt. Clerk in Holy Orders d. 1920' –

and then dallied in the herb garden. Sage, rosemary, hyssop and salad burnet, comfrey and clover. The domesticity suits the scale of the place. The gryphons squatting above the gables look too big for the house and have a predatory air which is mildly disconcerting. It is not palatial enough for quite such baronial decorations.

Presently the baronet returned and took us on a brief tour of the house. It felt polished and a little dark, with some of the orderly emptiness I associate with bachelor houses. It also feels impractical and has a marked Elizabethan lack of privacy about the bedrooms. It is a pre-corridor house. There are two spiral staircases and an impressive selection of four-poster beds, in one of which the politician Duncan Sandys was born. His father was MP for Wells.

The original owners were the Knoyle family. They were Roman Catholics who supported the King in the Civil War and then went on supporting the Stuarts after they were deposed. Not clever to be Catholics, Cavaliers and Jacobites. The poor Knoyles were three-time losers and in 1736 they sold Sandford Orcas to the Hutchings, who owned a larger, grander house in the nearby village of Milborne Port. They were not interested in the poor manor house, only in the farmland that went with it – about 450 acres. Until the early nineteenth century therefore it was let to tenant farmers.

In the nineteenth century Hubert Hutchings repossessed it and restored it, in the words of Lord David Cecil again, 'accurately and unobtrusively'. Lord David also says correctly that the words 'big' and 'great' are used relatively here. Although Sir

Mervyn and his ancestors talk of great chambers and big bedrooms there is really no such thing. Even 'the Great Hall' sits only a squashed eighty for the concerts Sir Mervyn puts on. It's still an elegant and unusual room, two sides of it taken up with mullioned bay windows decorated with stained-glass armorial bearings and reaching almost from floor to ceiling. But for the most part it is a warren of thick walled rooms and stone steps and stairs and original studded oak doors with keys to match.

Old Sir Hubert died in 1964 and Sir Mervyn, the present baronet, succeeded his uncle Christopher in 1986. Sir Christopher let it to a tenant, a retired colonel about whom Sir Mervyn had doubts. It was he who first let the public in and he made up endless apocryphal ghost stories with which to entertain them. Sir Mervyn mutters darkly about three-foot rapists and midnight harpsichord music. There IS a ghost at Sandford Orcas Manor, but it seems benign and consists of little more than shuffling footsteps in an empty room. There's really no need for invention. Eventually 'the Colonel' went. 'I persuaded him to leave, as the saying goes,' says Sir Mervyn.

And so, now, the Medlycotts are back in situ in their 'buried' house, tucked into the folds of the Dorset countryside. After the fête, Sir Mervyn told me, the house would 'quietly fall asleep till the village Christmas party.' The idea of a house sleeping is romantic to the point of fanciful, and yet in the case of Sandford Orcas Manor it seems quite apt.

In the Abbey that morning they had been singing the Nunc Dimittis. 'Lord now lettest thou thy servant depart in peace: according to thy word.' It reminded me, almost painfully, of old Sir Hubert on his knees, so old and not so far from death. And now it is Sir Mervyn's turn to mind the White Elephant stall, and draw the raffle and cosset the sleeping house.

'Big things ten p, small things five p.' Cream teas at £1.20. Comfrey and clover in the garden. A very English garden, a very English house, a uniquely English baronet.

VISITING THE HOUSES

Many of the houses are only open a few times a year. It is advisable
to write or telephone before arranging a visit.

Hagley Hall
Near Stourbridge
West Midlands
Tel: Hagley (0562) 882408

Goodwood House
Chichester
Sussex
Tel: Chichester (0243) 774107

Loseley House
Guildford
Surrey
Tel: Guildford (0483) 304440

Stansted Park
Rowlands Castle
West Sussex
Tel: (0705) 412265

Beaulieu
Beaulieu
Hampshire
Tel: Beaulieu (0590) 612345

Maunsel House
North Newton
Near Bridgwater
Somerset
Tel: (0278) 663413

Midelney Manor
Drayton
Near Langport
Somerset
Tel: not available.

Stratfield Saye House
Stratfield Saye
Reading
Berkshire
Tel: Basingstoke
(0256) 882882

Castle Howard
York
North Yorkshire
Tel: Coneysthorpe
(065384) 333

Bickleigh Castle
Near Tiverton
Devon
Tel: Bickleigh (08845) 363

Highclere Castle
Near Newbury
Hampshire
Tel: Highclere (0635) 253210

Milton Manor House
Near Abingdon
Oxfordshire
Tel: Abingdon (0235) 831287 or
831871

Sandringham House
Sandringham
Norfolk
Tel: King's Lynn
(0553) 772675

Somerleyton Hall
Near Lowestoft
Suffolk
Tel: Lowestoft
(0502) 730308

Ragley Hall
Alcester
Warwickshire
Tel: Alcester (0789) 762090

Gunby Hall
Burgh-le-Marsh
Lincolnshire
Tel: not available.

Hatfield House
Hatfield
Hertfordshire
Tel: Hatfield (0707) 262823

Brympton d'Evercy
Near Yeovil
Somerset
Tel: Yeovil (0935) 862528

Chatsworth
Bakewell
Derbyshire
Tel: Baslow (024658) 2204

Hartland Abbey
Bideford
North Devon
Tel: not available.

Weston Park
Near Shifnal
Shropshire
Tel: Weston-under-Lizard
(095276) 207

Styles
Styles
Devon
Tel: Dawlish (0626) 1

Sandford Orcas Manor
Sandford Orcas
Sherborne
Dorset
Tel: Corton Denham
(096322) 206